Business
as a Calling

Bringing Your Whole Self
(Body, Soul, and Spirit) to Work

DERICK MASENGALE

Business as a Calling: Bringing Your Whole Self (Body, Soul, and Spirit) to Work

Trilogy Christian Publishers
A Wholly Owned Subsidiary of Trinity Broadcasting Network
2442 Michelle Drive Tustin, CA 92780

Manufactured in the United States of America
10 9 8 7 6 5 4 3 2 1
Library of Congress Cataloging-in-Publication Data is available.

ISBN: 978-1-68556-496-4
E-ISBN: 978-1-68556-497-1

to Carol, Kyle, and Karli

ACKNOWLEDGMENTS

I would like to thank Pastor Brian Bales, pastor of Christian Fellowship Church in Ashburn, Virginia, for his encouragement to pursue putting this work together. Couldn't have done it without the confidence he helped me obtain through teaching the "Does Business Matter to God" course at Christian Fellowship Church. In addition, I would also like to thank all my colleagues that have contributed to my success throughout my career. Most importantly, I thank my Lord Jesus Christ for providing His grace and wisdom to guide me along my journey.

CONTENTS

PREFACE

Bringing your *whole self* to work is much discussed in corporate circles these days, usually in conjunction with diversity, equity, and inclusion in the workplace and society. All of these topics are important, yet at times it seems they don't apply to those whose viewpoints are based on the teachings of Christ. Because some find the name of Jesus offensive, believers are often discouraged from sharing their faith and, in some cases, prohibited from doing so in the workplace. It is a diversity of thought that some are unwilling to accept. While I am not advocating that believers overtly evangelize their workplaces, I do believe there is a need to bring our whole self to everything we do. For us believers, that means allowing our spiritual self to operate in all our day-to-day activities, including our professions.

Jesus taught that we are a spirit, we have a soul (made up of our mind, our will, and our emotions), and we live in a body. Based on this teaching, if we are to bring our whole self to work, we need to understand how to bring our body, soul, and *spirit* to our work. In our western culture, we invest hundreds of billions of dollars and countless hours annually to develop and care for our bodies. We have created an extensive educational system, and we invest hundreds of billions of dollars as well as untold hours in education to develop our mind and improve our mental health. Yet most Christians invest virtually no time in developing their spirit, and sadly, many are not aware of nor understand the benefits of doing so. If they are aware, an even smaller portion believes it is God's desire for them to develop their spirit and spiritual gifts to operate more effectively in their professions. This book makes a case for doing just that.

For those of us who recognize the importance of developing our spirit, the enemy is doing all he can to convince us the spiritual part of our beings must be suppressed as we interact with the world in the marketplace. His lies include, "It's okay to be spiritual in church, but don't bring it to your place of employment; it has no place there. The gifts of the Spirit are intended to support the ministry, not to support your career aspirations and progression." I submit that nothing could be further from the truth.

Followers of Christ have a critical place in the world of business and can bring their faith and spirituality to work to impact their businesses, co-workers, communities, and God. After all, Jesus directed His followers to be salt and light to the world, not in the church and to fellow believers, but out in the world. He wants us to bring who we are in Christ to engage and serve the world around us in every interaction.

This book is the result of my journey over multiple decades to reconcile my walk as a Spirit-filled follower of Christ with my career in business. Over my professional career, I have continued to study how to integrate the principles and teachings of Jesus with my professional goals and expectations. For years, I struggled to resolve questions like, "Can I really be serving God if I am not in full-time ministry?" "Could the roles I have in the marketplace be part of God's plan for me for furthering His kingdom?" "Or am I just chasing my own plans and dreams?" I didn't get answers to these questions in a day, a week, or a month. It took years, if not decades, to understand how God could and would use me to further His kingdom in my professional career. That is not to suggest I have it all figured out now; I am still learning. But I do have a peace and a better understanding of how to bring my body, soul, and spirit to my profession to serve the Lord, and in doing so, to have a positive impact on clients, co-workers, and my community.

As I wrestled with these and other related questions, I had to first settle in my mind whether God even cares about business. Was and am I spending my time and energy in an activity that God does not value and therefore is not worthy of my time? Maybe the answer to this question is obvious to you, but it wasn't to me. I needed to know if my ambition for success and my desire to have an impact and influence as a business leader was misplaced. Am I trying to apply my spiritual gifts and biblical truths to an unholy activity?

I knew from the study of the Bible that God cared about me and my success. I could see He was blessing my work, and I knew from Scripture that it was God's will to bless me, but I didn't consider what I was doing as a work fully devoted to God. Why? Because in my mind, it wasn't what I considered ministry work. How could it be right to use the gifts of the Spirit in a business setting? Consequently, I was constantly wondering if I was truly where God wanted me to be, and for a long time, I was never 100 percent certain that as I continued to learn and grow in my faith, it was okay to apply the spiritual truths I was learning to my business career and not a formal role in ministry.

Over the years, I saw many examples and heard many testimonies in church of individuals leaving their professions to take roles in full-time ministry, but it never seemed that God was leading me to do the same. Was I missing it? Did it mean I was not following His will because I was not in full-time ministry? I was working very hard to serve clients, my firm, and colleagues, but all the while not doing it under the banner of Christian ministry, and therefore, did it matter to God? I've provided financial support to ministries and charities delivering services to the poor and hurting but did not invest much of my time in direct ministry through the church. The fundamental questions I wrestled with were:

- Can I apply all I am learning about how to walk with God in His power if I am not in full-time ministry?
- Am I missing God and not walking in His plan but instead following my own plan because I enjoy what I am doing so much?

As I continued to look for answers to these questions, I finally decided I had to understand whether business matters to God. If it did, then being placed where I was and the blessings I was experiencing started to make sense. The only way I knew to do that was to find out what the Bible (the Word of God) had to say about working in a secular role. I needed the Word of God to confirm that I could have a ministry in the world of business, and if so, I could understand what that ministry might look like.

This book presents the results of my study and experience by providing the answers to these questions, which I found in Scripture, in prayer, and in practically applying them to the daily activities I encountered as a business professional. The book is organized into three sections:

1. God's Role for Business: we will explore what the Word of God has to say about business and commerce.
2. Spiritual Fundamentals: we will look at funda- mental biblical truths and why they are import-

ant to successfully execute our daily professional activities.

3. Applying the Fundamentals and Delivering Impact: we will look at practical examples of how to apply biblical truths and deliver impact for our businesses, colleagues, and community.

I have included many scriptural references for consideration with respect to each topic and question discussed. Whereas others have written volumes on each topic, in the pages of this book, I can only touch on each one. My prayer is that this book provides you with the scriptural basis to know it is God's will for you to succeed wherever He calls you, that He provides insight into how to bring your whole self to your profession, and that you recognize the unique impact you as a Spirit-filled follower of Christ can have on your colleagues, your business, your customers, and your community.

God's Role for Business

CHAPTER 1

Does Business Matter to God?

And God blessed them and said to them, Be fruitful, multiply, and fill the earth, and subdue it [using all its vast resources in the service of God and man]; and have dominion over the fish of the sea, the birds of the air, and over every living creature that moves upon the earth.

Genesis 1:28 (AMP)

To begin, let me provide a little background on my story. In 1985 I was in engineering school, and I was funding my education via a lawn maintenance company I started in Tampa, Florida. While that elevator pitch sounded good, if you looked deeper, you would've seen that I was failing at both my education and my business. I was living a lifestyle that was undisciplined and not consistent with the Word of God. Consequently, I was struggling in all areas of my life. All the sin I was living in produced the fruit of sin—confusion, lack of vision, failure, and frustration. I was miserable.

One day in the spring of 1985, I finally went to God and said, "Okay, if You are real, I need to know. I've tried many things, and none of them seem to work. I need to know if You and the Bible are real." Within a matter of weeks, God supernaturally placed ministries in my path that presented a message from the Bible that I had never heard before. Their message was that God cared about me, He cared about my success, and they encouraged me to study the Bible for myself to confirm it. As I studied, I found that the Bible was not a book of rules as religion presents it (and how it had been taught to me), but, in fact, it is a book of promises—promises I could base my life decisions on. Over time, as I learned more and made better decisions—decisions based on principles laid out in the Bible—I started to see the results of those decisions manifest positive results in my life: less confusion, a developing vision, and small successes along the way. That proof was all I needed to believe that God and His Word are real and alive. It made me hungry to learn as much as I could about the truths presented in the Bible.

I found that the Bible was not a book of rules as religion presents it but, in fact, it is a book of promises.

My situation didn't change overnight; however, my attitude did. It changed from someone who had a very negative outlook on life to someone who could see good possibilities in every situation. I started to expect good things to happen, and little by little, my circumstances changed to the point where many years later, I can call myself a blessed man.

One of the first revelations God provided me was that religious activity and faith are not synonymous. The terms "Christian religion" and "Christian faith" are often used interchangeably in our society today. Yet, as I studied, I found they are, in fact, polar opposites. Religion looks at the Bible as a book of rules we must keep. Faith looks at the Bible as a book of promises we must believe and receive. Religion tells us that if we want God to love and bless us, we must master all kinds of rules and regulations, and if we don't, God will not be happy with us. Faith tells us that God loves us while we are sinners, and no matter what we've done or will do, His love toward us does not change.

We get in a right relationship with God, through grace, by faith in the redemptive work Jesus did at the cross. It is a gift; we can't earn it. We must take it by faith, just like every other promise in the Word of God. That revelation changed my thinking and perspective forever. I began to see God as a father who loved me, not as one looking to punish me because I didn't master all the rules. That simple truth was the switch that flipped my attitude and outlook.

I dove into the Word of God to find the promises He made to those who follow Him. I took many of those promises as personal. I saw myself as a child of God and knew it was God's will to bless me, not because of anything I did, but because of what Jesus did at the cross—His sacrifice. I also found in the Word that God gives all of us specific gifts and talents, and it was my responsibility to work with the Holy Spirit to discover what mine are and to develop them to achieve God's plan for my life.

Over the years, God has provided several professional opportunities for me to further develop the gifts and talents He provided me and to see God's hand blessing my work as I developed those gifts. As I continued to learn, I still struggled with the question, "Should I be applying these godly principles and truths to my professional career? Shouldn't they be applied in a ministry of some kind?" I couldn't clearly connect what I was doing daily with a higher purpose of ministry. It seemed that whatever ministry was, it should be more than applying the biblical principles to how I performed my job.

I've been attending church for more than thirty years now, and I haven't seen a lot of teaching from the pulpit about what a ministry in the business world looks like. This is not a criticism; it just describes my experience. The times it was discussed, it was in terms of overtly witnessing about Jesus to co-workers. I'd seen many examples of Christians doing that so poorly (more on this later) that I didn't really want to be associated with it. Quite frankly, I think God has only asked me to do that a handful of times over the years, and the other person always initiated the conversation. I did not just walk up and tell them.

So, I continued to develop my faith and seek success in the business world. In my profession, business and technology consulting, becoming a partner/managing director is a measure of that success and a title that many strive to obtain. However, as I was going through the final steps to become a managing director, I realized the partner/managing director role was not the culmination of what God had for me. It was only the means to something more. As I was approaching that milestone, I spent the months leading up to that promotion in prayer about how God would use me in that role.

One Sunday morning, I got the time mixed up and arrived at church an hour early. To this day, I don't know how I did that, but it turned out to be a significant waypoint for me in my journey. When I realized I was early, I wandered into the bookstore to pass the time and found a book entitled *Every Good Endeavor* by Timothy Keller. Keller pastors in New York City, and many Wall Street investors, attorneys, and young professionals attend his church. His book is about ministering to those professionals and how they can have an impact in the business world for Jesus. While I was waiting for the service to start, I read through the first thirty to forty pages and got the sense that this could be where God was leading me. Over the next few months,

I read a number of books on the topic, listed on his website, and spent time praying about what to do next.

Eventually, I mustered up the courage to send a note to my pastor, saying, "I think God may be leading me to pull together a class around business being a calling." I was very hesitant, but he and I had a few discussions, and he encouraged me to pursue the idea. So, I spent the next few months putting together the content for a class titled "Does Business Matter to God?" The content for that class turned out to be the basis for this book.

As I started to shape the class, I needed to find God's view of business in the Bible. If you want to know God's will for a situation, the first place to start is His Word—the Bible. So, the first question I asked when considering business as a calling was, "What is God's view of work?" When I looked in the Word of God, I found He commanded man to work. Genesis 2:15 (AMP) states: "And the Lord God took the man and put him in the Garden of Eden to tend and guard and keep it."

We can see in this scripture that God didn't put man (the species of man, men and women) in the garden to be passive. He gave man a job when He placed him in the garden: tend the garden and keep it. That takes work. Another key thing we learn when studying Genesis is that God worked. We all know the famous scripture in Genesis 2:2 (AMP): "And on the seventh day God ended His work which He had done; and He rested on the seventh day from all His work which He had done."

So if God worked, work is certainly not some unholy activity. Furthermore, He wasn't working at ministry; He was creating. That may seem obvious, but I needed to settle it based on what the Word of God said. I also found that God didn't just create everything and then stopped working. Scripture tells us that God still works today. The scriptural evidence of that is found in Isaiah

64:4 (AMP): "For from of old no one has heard nor perceived by the ear, nor has the eye seen a God besides You, Who works and shows Himself active on behalf of him who [earnestly] waits for Him."

He is constantly working and showing Himself active on our behalf. I suggest the evidence of this in our lives is directly proportional to the time we spend seeking Him—earnestly waiting. In John 5:17 (AMP), Jesus Himself clearly makes the point that God is working today: "But Jesus answered them, My Father has worked [even] until now, [He has never ceased working; He is still working] and I, too, must be at [divine] work."

So, too, we are commanded to be at God's work. However, is God's idea of work for us associated only with ministry through the institution of the church? We are all members of the body of Christ, but are we all called to work in an office of the institution known as the church? For me, that was the next big question because I always associated ministry with the church. Did I need to have a ministry role in the institution of the church to use the spiritual truths I was learning? It is clear from Scripture that we are to engage with the church, be part of the local assembly of the body, and provide financial, physical, and prayer support to the mission of the church. But is that a ministry?

Through my study, I have come to realize that everyone is called, but not everyone is called to be engaged in the business of the institution of the church. Why do I say that? Let's look at Scripture to see what the Word says. In Scripture, God has given us the mandate to fill, subdue, and tend to the earth in the service of God and man. This is often referred to as the "Genesis Mandate" and found in Genesis 1:28 (AMP):

And God blessed them and said to them, Be fruitful, multiply, and fill the earth, and subdue it [using all its vast resources in the service of God and man]; and have dominion over the fish of the sea, the birds of the air, and over every living creature that moves upon the earth.

We can see in this scripture that God has called man to take the resources He has provided and serve both Himself and man with those resources (people and raw materials). It is easy to see a significant role for business to play in that command. After all, businesses continually take raw materials and convert them into products that improve the quality of life for all of us. Where would we be without the ability to easily obtain clothing, housing, food, and transportation? Each of these is available because someone had a vision for a business—a group of people with a common objective, to take raw materials and create a product or service to meet a need or desire of the community around them. For those of us who have a vocation not directly related to the ministry of the church, how does our vocation today align with this mandate? It is helpful to take a look at what vocation really means. *Vocation* comes from the Latin word *vocare*, meaning "to

> *We can see in this scripture that God has called man to take the resources He has provided and serve both God and man with those resources.*

call." Is our professional vocation really a calling? Does God call us into a vocation that is not directly tied to the church?

In his book, *Every Good Endeavor*, Timothy Keller asserts, "A job is a vocation only if someone else calls you to do it and you do it for them rather than for yourself. Based on this definition, our work can be a calling only if it is reimagined as a mission of service to something beyond merely our own interests."[1] That sounds a bit like a call to ministry (the act of serving others), doesn't it? This view provides one way to assess if we are engaged in a God-directed vocation or if we just have a job. To make that determination, one can start by asking the following questions:

1. How much input did God have in me taking the position I am in? Did He call me to this position/role? Did I even ask Him? Does He care where I work?
2. Do I see my role as a role of service, and if so, to whom?

When considering these questions, I'm reminded of the beginning of Rick Warren's book, *The Purpose Driven Life*, where it says, "It's not about you."[2] I submit that our roles in business as followers of Christ are not about us but about serving others. As we often do, I took a simple concept, made it complicated, and, as a result, created confusion. My definition of ministry was being shaped by observing pastoral ministries, teaching ministries, evangelical outreach ministries—all full-time activities focused on sharing God and His Word with others.

I could easily see how important spiritual gifts and God's truths are to the success of those activities. But I struggled to convince myself it was okay to bring those spiritual gifts into the

Business as a Calling | Derick Masengale

roles I had in the marketplace. As with so many things, one day, the simplicity of it finally dawned on me. I was led by the Holy Spirit to look up the definition of the word *ministry* and found that it means simply "to serve others." God has called me, us, into a position to serve others—to be salt and to bring light. And guess what? I don't have to be in a formal ministry position in the church to do it. I realized serving others in my vocation can be and is a full-time ministry role that requires applying Bible-based principles and truths for success.

This is a concept so simple, and yet it took me years to understand. God calls us to a place where we can serve, and He equips us with the talents and gifts to walk successfully in that vocation (calling) so that we can serve with impact. With that understanding, it is incumbent upon us to determine if we are in the position He designed us for and called us to.

As you consider this perspective, I want to spend a minute sharing some personal experience and observations. What we are going to explore is something much deeper than just witnessing about Jesus to people in the workplace. I have seen multiple instances in my career where those who confessed their faith in Jesus to everyone were some of the laziest and most unreliable workers in the office. They were completely unaware that they had zero credibility with those they were trying to witness to and that, from their example, many didn't want to have anything to do with the Jesus they followed. This is tragic.

These people had good intentions, and I am sure they really cared for their co-workers, yet they were ineffective in sharing the gospel. They may not have been mature enough to view their roles as roles in ministry and therefore may not have consistently served those around them before witnessing.

As followers of Christ, we should be bringing a level of excellence and service to the workplace that others recognize, value, and respect. If God has placed you in your vocation, Scripture tells us He equips you with all spiritual gifts to accomplish what you need to be successful in that role. That also means success at being a witness for Jesus, not just witnessing about Jesus. Those are two very different things. One shows; the other tells. People want to see; they don't just want to hear.

Before we can witness effectively in the workplace, those we work with need to see us as people of high integrity, consistently committed to doing our jobs as well as we can, committed to the success of those around us, and committed to success of the organization. We must continue to look for opportunities to serve (minister to) those around us. Ministry is not about telling them about Jesus all the time. It is about serving them and putting their interests ahead of ours to develop relationships built on trust.

People are looking for someone to trust. They are watching us, and the little things we do matter. I was working for a client, and we were evaluating software products to determine which would be the best fit to meet my client's business requirements. We were coming to the end of the evaluation period, and we had determined which product we would recommend, but we had not yet sat down with the client and walked through the results of the evaluation. I had made a commitment to the client not to share the results with anyone until we had reviewed the results with them first. We scheduled the review for a Monday.

On the Friday before, I received a call from one of the product vendors asking if I could share the results of the evaluation. It just so happened he represented the product we were going to recommend. As soon as he asked the question, I sensed the Holy Spirit reminding me I had given my word to the client that I would not share the results. So, I told him I could not share the results until I reviewed them with the client. He was very disappointed and, as a result, pushed back a bit and stated his conclusion that because I would not share the results, his firm must not have been selected. I reiterated that I couldn't share results until I had spoken with the client, and much to his disappointment, we ended the call. I met with the client the following Monday and reviewed the results. I then called the sales representative and told him the good news that his product was recommended. However, that is not the end of the story.

He worked for a global firm, and a couple of months later, I got a call from the firm's vice president of U.S. sales located on the other side of the country. After a polite exchange of hellos and how are yous, he said, "You know, Derick, you have quite a reputation within our firm."

I was thinking, *Why would that be?* So, I said, "Really? Why?"

He said, "You are viewed as having a high level of integrity and someone we can trust."

I was a bit surprised and said, "Really? Why is that?"

He then replayed the story I just shared with you back to me and told me how that impacted their sales organization at the national level. It reaffirmed for me how important everything I do is. People are watching. They notice, and they don't forget. As I said earlier, people are looking for those they can trust. They are looking for competent people who are not just looking out for their own self-interest.

That example was prompted by the Holy Spirit to remind me of the commitment I had made. The good news is that I listened. The result had an impact on an entire group of salespeople and created a relationship built on trust that I leveraged for other clients and other business deals over subsequent years. Furthermore, it reaffirmed for me that God cares about our vocations and how we walk and serve in our positions. After all, He called me to the role, and His Holy Spirit prompted me during the interaction with that sales representative.

He will use us to serve (minister to) others by placing us in positions of increasing influence, and His Holy Spirit will guide us to do it well if we listen and let Him. This is why we must bring our "spiritual self" to our professions. God is a Spirit, and if we want to hear from Him, we must use our spirit to hear His Spirit speak to us. We will explore how to do this in much more detail throughout this book.

As followers of Jesus, it is important for us to continually become more skillful at what we do and be an example of God's integrity and trustworthiness to those around us. That consistency of service and excellence will have people asking us how we are able to operate as we do. In difficult times, how do we keep a positive outlook and show others respect even when it's not reciprocated? When asked, as God leads, we can then share the gospel from a place of power based on the respect and influence we have earned through building trust and working to make others successful.

You might be thinking, *That all sounds great, but I'm just a janitor or a short-order cook. I wouldn't call what I do a vocation.* If God has called you into that role, for now, it is a vocation. He is using that role to prepare you for the next. We all start from a place of little or no vocational power or influence. It is important to recognize that true and lasting influence is not based on titles. It is based on trusted relationships, and those relationships only develop over time. I have seen multiple examples of those who strove for a title, and once they got there, they found their influence hadn't really changed. Why? Because they didn't take time to build the trusted relationships along their journey for continued success. They thought their titles motivated others to work for and with them.

Small beginnings are nothing to be ashamed of. God has made a promise to us in Matthew 25:21 (AMP):

> *His master said to him, Well done, you upright (honorable, admirable) and faithful servant! You have been faithful and trustworthy over a little; I will put you in charge of much. Enter into and share the joy (the delight, the blessedness) which your master enjoys.*

When we keep up our end by being faithful over little, by continuing to put others first, and by striving for excellence independent of the role we are in, we are preparing ourselves for the time when God will deliver on His promise to make us rulers over much. To truly operate in the impactful role God desires for us, it is important for our character to be developed. God often tests and develops our character while being faithful over little, and the resulting maturity takes time and patience.

My study and experience made it clear to me that God has called people to the business world, and He wants to use us to minister to those around us—those who may never walk into a church. It is up to us to learn how to stay aligned with His leading as we navigate our careers and as our influence increases. Until I got the revelation of what ministry is, I always had a nagging thought that if I wasn't in a formal church role, I may not be doing what God wanted even though I could see I was being blessed and I was able to bless others. Now, I no longer wonder if I can have a ministry while operating in the business world, and I now have a much better idea of what ministering in the business world looks like.

Going back to Genesis 1:28 and the direction provided by that scripture, what does it look like to use the vast resources God provides to serve man and Him? It could be:

- Developing the next big app that helps organize our busy lives
- Writing the next *New York Times* best-selling novel for others to enjoy
- Developing the next wave of technical innovation to create jobs and opportunities for thousands of people
- Opening a local restaurant and creating a place for family and friends to spend time together
- Owning a contracting business that does high-quality work at a fair price

Businesses provide a mechanism to fulfill the vision God laid out in the Genesis Mandate: to use the resources God provides to create a product or service that blesses man in a way that blesses God. It takes people led by the Holy Spirit to guide the work in a way that blesses man and God, not just themselves.

Do you view your vocation that way? Only those who bring their whole self—body, soul, and spirit—can achieve this goal. Do you see your vocation as a calling, and are you using your position and influence to bless and serve others, or are you using it to bless yourself? From the Word, it is clear that God's desire is for us to work. More importantly, God has said He will bless our work. Deuteronomy 30:9 (AMP) says: "And the Lord your God will make you abundantly prosperous in every work of your hand, in the fruit of your body, of your cattle, of your land, for good; for the Lord will again delight in prospering you, as He took delight in your fathers."

That is great news and a topic we will discuss in more detail throughout this book. God blesses our work, and we can trust that He is in control of our careers if we allow Him to be so. In fact, He delights in it. After all, He is doing the calling, and He is calling us to positions that allow us to bless others. In order to do that, He needs to bless us first.

I encourage you to find out where God is calling you. *He is* calling you somewhere. He has a calling for everyone, and it will be in a role of ministry—in the service of others. In the next chapter, we will explore in more detail why God is calling some to a career in business.

CHAPTER 2

Why Does God Call Some to the Business World?

And the Levite [because he has no part or inheritance with you] and the stranger or temporary resident, and the fatherless and the widow who are in your towns shall come and eat and be satisfied, so that the Lord your God may bless you in all the work of your hands that you do.

Deuteronomy 14:29 (AMP)

Why would God call some of His people to a vocation in business? Is it only so we can acquire the resources to sustain ourselves and our families? Is it to provide personal satisfaction by offering an opportunity to use the gifts and talents He has equipped us with, or in addition to these things, is there a higher purpose?

God does not have small thoughts, and His purposes for us are not small. Even if He has called us into something that looks small, when He blesses it, it turns into something impactful. Mother Teresa was not looking for fame; she was just trying to meet the needs of those abandoned in one small place in the world. Her goal was to love them. Her view was, "Not all of us can do great things, but we can do small things with great love." She lived a meager existence by our western standards, yet she became one of the most respected and influential persons of her time. God prospered the work she did and increased her influence as she remained faithful to her calling. While it was not a role in the business world, it is a tremendous example of how God prospers the work He has called His people to do.

At the end of the last chapter, I shared Deuteronomy 30:9 (AMP): "And the Lord your God will make you abundantly prosperous in every work of your hand, in the fruit of your body, of your cattle, of your land, for good; for the Lord will again delight in prospering you, as He took delight in your fathers."

That is God's promise to His sons and daughters. It makes Him happy to prosper His people. What an awesome thing to know. If we are in God's will, in the vocation He has destined for us, it is His will to bless all the works of our hands. That includes not just a financial blessing; it also includes increasing our level of influence. Mother Teresa was not seeking it, but her level of influence ultimately exceeded many of the most powerful people of her time. While many world leaders of the day spent their lives striving for power, she spent her time loving the abandoned yet found herself with a level of influence that exceeded many of those who had spent their entire lives pursuing it. She remained faithful to God's calling for her, and God responded by remaining faithful to the promises in His Word to bless the works of her hands.

As God prospers us, He also expects some things from us. Deuteronomy 14:28–29 says:

> *At the end of every three years you shall bring forth all the tithe of your increase the same year and lay it up within your towns. And the Levite [because he has no part or inheritance with you] and the stranger or temporary resident, and the fatherless and the widow who are in your towns shall come and eat and be satisfied,*

so that the Lord your God may bless you in all the work
of your hands that you do.

To continue experiencing God's blessing on the works of our hands, He clearly says He expects us to bring our tithe as a form of worship and to support the works of God to aid the less fortunate. From the spiritual perspective, we tithe to be obedient to God's Word and most importantly worship the Lord with it. Tithing is an act of worship. We thank Him for blessing us and remind ourselves that all good comes from God. God promises in His Word that if we tithe, He will "rebuke the devourer for our sake." He promises to keep the enemy from taking what we have, which in turn allows us to continue experiencing God's blessings.

I also believe that tithing is fundamental to allowing God to work in our finances. He has promised that He will open the storehouse of heaven and pour out His blessings upon us. What a promise. Another important and practical aspect of tithing is that it helps keep us from being covetous and lusting after more money and more things—just for the sake of money and things. Our willingness to always give a portion of what we have directly opposes the tendency to covet, hoard, and trust in the riches. It requires us to trust God instead. As God continues to bless us, the temptations to covet and lust after things do not go away, and our willingness to give our tithe first helps defeat those temptations. Deuteronomy 24:18–19 (AMP) says:

> *But you shall [earnestly] remember that you were a*
> *slave in Egypt and the Lord your God redeemed you*
> *from there; therefore I command you to do this. When*
> *you reap your harvest in your field and have forgotten a*
> *sheaf in the field, you shall not go back to get it; it shall*

be for the stranger and the sojourner, the fatherless, and the widow, that the Lord your God may bless you in all the work of your hands.

These verses also speak to giving of our increase to the poor. The Bible often refers to this as the giving of alms. On a personal note, my wife and I tithed from the day we were married, but it wasn't until fifteen or so years later that we also began giving alms. I don't believe it was a coincidence that our income increased dramatically and has continued to grow as we have continued to give more to support the poor and hurting in addition to our tithe. The Bible teaches we should not seek to store up all our increase (i.e., building bigger barns or storehouses), but that we should be watchful and willing to give to those less fortunate. God blesses us so that we can bless others; however, we are not just working for others. God also expects us to enjoy our work and His blessings. Ecclesiastes 5:18–19 (AMP) says:

Behold, what I have seen to be good and fitting is for one to eat and drink, and to find enjoyment in all the labor in which he labors under the sun all the days which God gives him—for this is his [allotted] part. Also, every man to whom God has given riches and possessions, and the power to enjoy them and to accept his appointed lot and to rejoice in his toil—this is the gift of God [to him].

God has also promised us that we can find enjoyment in our labor. He has given us the power to enjoy our possessions and enjoy our work. This is His desire. This is an area where the enemy can get us sideways in our thinking. Have you ever felt guilty because you enjoy what you do, and when you hear stories about how someone has given up all to serve in the church or on the mission field, you think to yourself, *I'm not sacrificing enough, I must not be in the will of God because I'm blessed, I enjoy what I do, and I am not sacrificing like others?*

It is God's will to enjoy our work and the blessings that come with it.

Just because God has called some to the mission field, that doesn't mean He has called you. If He hasn't called you, He hasn't provided you the grace to perform and enjoy that assignment. You would be toiling in that work. We need to seek God to find out where He wants us to serve and do it, irrespective of what others think and the "guilt" you may feel. This scripture tells us it is God's will to enjoy our work and the blessings that come with it. It is His gift to us. It is His will for us to prosper financially as a result of our work, and it is also His will and our responsibility to increase in our skill. But there is more. Let's look at Proverbs 22:29 (AMP): "Do you see a man diligent and skillful in his business? He will stand before kings; he will not stand before obscure men."

Another key for us to be blessed in business is found in this scripture: we must be skillful and diligent. His blessing and our success will not just fall on us because we go to church, pray, and read the Bible. We have a very active role in developing our skill so we are prepared for the roles He desires for us. This scripture provides insight into the influence God wants us to have. If we are diligent and skillful in our business, we will stand before kings. Sounds pretty influential to me. While all of us may not stand before kings, we will stand before influential leaders. It could be leaders within your organization, community, or church. Why?

Because with that influence, we are positioned to better leverage our skills and experiences to bless others and love them as God loves us.

It is clear from Scripture that God has called some to business. God has a plan for His people to participate in commerce and to bless them in their vocation. It is important for us to recognize this and to seek God so that:

- We know which role He wants us in
- God can bless us through our work so we can be a blessing to others

The reality of the world we live in is that commerce generates the wealth to pay all the taxes that fund our governments, the wealth to provide financial support for social charities, and the wealth to provide financial support for spreading the gospel. How could God not have called men and women to take positions in business to be conduits for moving the wealth of the world into His mission of spreading the gospel and helping the poor? Do you view your role in business as a calling?

In his book *Why Business Matters to God*,[3] Van Duzer asserts the purpose for business is to:

1. Provide goods and services that will allow a community to flourish
2. Serve employees by providing them with opportunities to express at least a portion of their God-given identity through meaningful, creative work

As I struggled to articulate what God was revealing to me, I read this definition of purpose and thought, *That's it!* That succinctly summarized what God had put into my spirit. It has subsequently helped frame my perspective on how to have a ministry and an impact as a business leader. When I view business through these two lenses, I can see why it is important to succeed in business by increasing my influence and why that would matter to God. Both purposes presented above are focused on service (ministry) to others, not on serving myself. My success is not about me. It is about how I can bless others with the services and products I am responsible for delivering and for opportunities I can provide to employees of my firm to grow professionally and reach their God-given potential.

It is up to us to pray and work with God to make sure we are in the roles He desires for us and to look at our employment as a calling (vocation) and not just a job. As Rick Warren stated, "It is not about us." It's not just about enriching ourselves. It is about providing goods and services to help the community flourish and providing employees with opportunities to express their God-given talents and gifts. Do you believe your position in the marketplace is where God has called you? If so, are you operating in that role like it is a call of service to others? What might that look like? It comes down to how we operate (what is our witness) daily:

- Do those who work with you view you as a person of integrity?
- Do those around you notice that you have a peace amid turmoil?

- Do you believe God provides wisdom and insight to help you successfully navigate the challenges of the workplace?
- Do you care about the well-being of those around you?
- Do you get joy from your work?

God's goal for us is not to be the highest-paid individual within our firms, within our industries, or within our cities or states. That may happen; however, it is *What is your motivation? Is it to earn more and obtain titles or is it to gain wealth and influence to further God's desire to help the hurting in your community?* about the influence you have and the impact you make with it. As we discussed in the last chapter, influence is earned over time as you develop trusted relationships. Years of influence can be wiped out in a flash through unwise decisions, most of which are based on selfishness and fear.

We have a laundry list of examples of those who used their influence to meet their selfish desires. Jeffrey Skilling, Kenneth Lay, Michael Milken, and Bernie Madoff all had great success, followed by tremendous failure. Most importantly, their falls didn't just impact them. They had a crushing impact on hundreds of thousands of people and entire communities. They viewed the purpose of business as a mechanism to allow them to amass wealth and power. It was about them. The more influence you obtain, the bigger your impact can be, both positively and negatively. What is your motivation? Is it to earn more and obtain titles, or is it to gain wealth and influence to further God's desire to help the hurting in your community?

As we will discuss later in this book, it is God's will for us to prosper, but we will need to stay connected closely to Him so we don't find ourselves drifting into an area where we are focused on self and off the path He has for us. It is a constant struggle. As we gain influence, the enemy will work twice as hard to cause us to break the trust the influence is built upon and, as a result, minimize our influence and discredit our witness and faith in God. There will be times when things are not moving as fast as we would like, and the enemy will use those times to try and cloud our vision, get our focus off God, and get us to compromise. It is up to us to continue to spend time with God to keep the vision clear even when circumstances around us are not.

Let's look at Scripture to see two examples of leaders who remained faithful during extremely trying times. We'll see how they held on to their vision and the impact their faithfulness ultimately had on an entire nation and region of the world. We are going to look at the accounts of Joseph and Daniel. Both biographies follow a similar pattern:

- They were anointed, had God's favor upon them, were seen as skillful in their roles, and reached a place of success by the world's standards
- Their faith was tested through unfair and unjust circumstances
- They remained faithful as they suffered through difficult circumstances
- They were restored to positions of greater authority and influence

- They used their positions of influence to bless huge numbers of people

Let's look at their stories, starting with Joseph:

> *But the Lord was with Joseph, and he [though a slave] was a successful and prosperous man; and he was in the house of his master the Egyptian. And his master saw that the Lord was with him and that the Lord made all that he did to flourish and succeed in his hand. So Joseph pleased [Potiphar] and found favor in his sight, and he served him. And [his master] made him supervisor over his house and he put all that he had in his charge. From the time that he made him supervisor in his house and over all that he had, the Lord blessed the Egyptian's house for Joseph's sake; and the Lord's blessing was on all that he had in the house and in the field.*
>
> Genesis 39:2–5 (AMP)

Joseph was a slave, yet he didn't view himself as such. He was a successful and prosperous man, even as a slave. More importantly, his master saw the reasons for his success; it was because the Lord was with him, and He was the one who prospered Joseph. Key point here: scripture doesn't say that Joseph told his master about his God, but it does say that Potiphar figured it out by watching Joseph perform his daily duties. Joseph found favor and trust in his master's sight because he was skillful and blessed in all that he did, and as a result, Potiphar prospered, and his house was blessed. The Word says that God will do the same for each of us. As we seek Him, He will bless the works of our hands so much that others around us will notice and be blessed—a very powerful witness.

Let's look at Daniel.

> *And in all matters of wisdom and understanding concerning which the king asked them, he found them ten times better than all the [learned] magicians and enchanters who were in his whole realm.*
>
> Daniel 1:20 (AMP)

> *Then the king made Daniel great and gave him many great gifts, and he made him to rule over the whole province of Babylon and to be chief governor over all the wise men of Babylon.*
>
> Daniel 2:48 (AMP)

> *It pleased [King] Darius [successor to Belshazzar] to set over the kingdom 120 satraps who should be [in charge] throughout all the kingdom, and over them three presidents—of whom Daniel was one—that these satraps might give account to them and that the king should have no loss or damage. Then this Daniel was distinguished above the presidents and the satraps because an excellent spirit was in him, and the king thought to set him over the whole realm.*
>
> Daniel 6:1–3 (AMP)

The king saw Daniel as one who had unmatched wisdom and knowledge, one who provided great insight to him and helped him prosper. He saw an excellent spirit in Daniel and set him in charge of the whole realm. As a result, the king gave Daniel many gifts and a position of great influence.

In both examples, others could see that Daniel and Joseph possessed unmatched wisdom and produced excellent results. They were highly valued by their leaders. No matter what role we may currently have (remember Joseph was a slave), if we seek God's wisdom and walk in His ways, He will bless us, provide us wisdom to do our work with excellence, and enable us to be a blessing to those around us and help them prosper. That is His promise to us. As He blesses us, people will notice because they are blessed, as well.

As Daniel and Joseph prospered, they were soon falsely accused and suffered great harm from those who were jealous of their success. This aligns perfectly with the words of Jesus in Mark 10:30 (AMP), "Who will not receive a hundred times as much now in this time—houses and brothers and sisters and mothers and children and lands, with persecutions—and in the age to come, eternal life." If God is blessing us, Jesus says we can expect to be persecuted. The enemy will do all he can to try and destroy our witness. The persecution proved to be a great test of Daniel and Joseph's integrity and character.

> *Then after a time his master's wife cast her eyes upon Joseph, and she said, Lie with me. But he refused and said to his master's wife, See here, with me in the house my master has concern about nothing; he has put all that he has in my care. He is not greater in this house than I am; nor has he kept anything from me except you, for you are his wife. How then can I do this great evil and sin against God? She spoke to Joseph day after*

day, but he did not listen to her, to lie with her or to be
with her.

Genesis 39:7–10 (AMP)

Then she told him the same story, saying, The Hebrew
servant whom you brought among us came to me to
mock and insult me. And when I screamed and cried,
he left his garment with me and fled out [of the house].
And when [Joseph's] master heard the words of his wife,
saying to him, This is the way your servant treated me,
his wrath was kindled. And Joseph's master took him
and put him in the prison, a place where the state pris-
oners were confined; so he was there in the prison.

Genesis 39:17–20 (AMP)

It is interesting that Joseph didn't see the request from his master's wife as an act against his master even though it clearly would have been. He saw it as an act against God. There is a message in that statement. Some actions that are acceptable to those around us *we know* are not acceptable to God. Will we stand our ground in those situations?

Joseph stood his ground and remained a man of integrity. Yet, he was falsely accused and thrown into prison for that very act. Talk about a disappointment! He did the honorable thing and the right thing in God's sight, only to find himself in prison. He could have easily shifted his thinking and blamed God for not protecting him. After all, he did what he knew was God's will and was thrown into prison anyway. How could that be God's will? Worse yet, if it was, would you want to follow a God like that?

I'm sure many of us have been mistreated or falsely accused by individuals we interact with in our daily business activities. How did we react? Were there times when you thought God had turned His back on your situation? For me, there was more than one time that things took an unexpected turn, and I wondered what was happening to me and the vision I was certain God had given me. Things were not playing out as I had expected, and I couldn't understand how what was happening could possibly be God's will.

I mention this to share a truth: as you are blessed and your influence increases, it will come with persecution. God's Word declares it. You can bet the challenges will become even more pronounced, and the stakes associated with the decisions you make on how to respond will be even higher as your influence grows. Joseph did the right thing, and his situation immediately got worse. Daniel suffered a similar wrong.

> *Then the presidents and satraps sought to find occasion [to bring accusation] against Daniel concerning the kingdom, but they could find no occasion or fault, for he was faithful, nor was there any error or fault found in him. Then said these men, We shall not find any occasion [to bring accusation] against this Daniel except we find it against him concerning the law of his God. Then these presidents and satraps came [tumultuously] together to the king and said to him, King Darius, live forever! All the presidents of the kingdom, the deputies and the satraps, the counselors and the governors, have consulted and agreed that the king should establish a royal statute and make a firm decree that whoever shall ask a petition of any god or man*

for thirty days, except of you, O king, shall be cast into the den of lions. Now, O king, establish the decree and sign the writing that it may not be changed, according to the law of the Medes and Persians, which cannot be altered. So King Darius signed the writing and the decree. Now when Daniel knew that the writing was signed, he went into his house, and his windows being open in his chamber toward Jerusalem, he got down upon his knees three times a day and prayed and gave thanks before his God, as he had done previously. Then these men came thronging [by agreement] and found Daniel praying and making supplication before his God. Then they came near and said before the king concerning his prohibitory decree, Have you not signed an edict that any man who shall make a petition to any god or man within thirty days, except of you, O king, shall be cast into the den of lions? The king answered and said, The thing is true, according to the law of the Medes and Persians, which cannot be changed or repealed. Then they said before the king, That Daniel, who is one of the exiles from Judah, does not regard or pay any attention to you, O king, or to the decree that you have signed, but makes his petition three times a day. Then the king, when he heard these words, was much distressed [over what he had done] and set his mind on Daniel to deliver him; and he labored until the sun went down to rescue him. Then these same men came thronging [by agreement] to the king and said, Know, O king, that it is a law of the Medes and Persians that no decree or statute which the king establishes may be changed or repealed. Then the

*king commanded, and Daniel was brought and cast
into the den of lions. The king said to Daniel, May
your God, Whom you are serving continually, deliver
you!*

Daniel 6:4–16 (AMP)

Talk about being mistreated! It is one thing to be attacked by those who are jealous of you and hate you because of your success. But being persecuted and condemned for seeking God is another level of attack. What was Daniel thinking? *How can this be God's will? What is going on here? God, I was honoring You and seeking You, and it is the very thing that has me condemned to death.* That could cause one to walk away from God.

It is interesting, though, that Daniel didn't even try to hide the fact that he prayed and had a relationship with God. The passage above says he left his windows open when he prayed. If he had closed his windows, the other leaders might not have been able to catch him in the act and accuse him.

Daniel could have also waited the thirty days before praying. However, could it be that he saw the constant communication with God as fundamental to successfully operating in his role for the king? What would we do if our job were threatened because of our faith? Would we blame God and turn our backs on Him to preserve our livelihood, or would we trust that God has our backs? If we are where God put us, He has promised that His protection will be on us. Let's see what Joseph and Daniel did.

Joseph:

*But the Lord was with Joseph, and showed him mercy
and loving-kindness and gave him favor in the sight of*

the warden of the prison. And the warden of the prison
committed to Joseph's care all the prisoners who were
in the prison; and whatsoever was done there, he was
in charge of it. The prison warden paid no attention to
anything that was in [Joseph's] charge, for the Lord was
with him and made whatever he did to prosper.

Genesis 39:21–23 (AMP)

Then Pharaoh sent and called Joseph, and they brought
him hastily out of the dungeon. But Joseph [first]
shaved himself, changed his clothes, and made himself
presentable; then he came into Pharaoh's presence.

Genesis 41:14 (AMP)

Daniel:

Then the king arose very early in the morning and
went in haste to the den of lions. And when he came
to the den and to Daniel, he cried out in a voice of
anguish. The king said to Daniel, O Daniel, servant of
the living God, is your God, Whom you serve contin-
ually, able to deliver you from the lions? Then Daniel
said to the king, O king, live forever! My God has sent
His angel and has shut the lions' mouths so that they
have not hurt me, because I was found innocent and
blameless before Him; and also before you, O king, [as
you very well know] I have done no harm or wrong.

Daniel 6:19–22 (AMP)

The Scripture shows that God was with them through their trials and delivered them. God's Word says He does not leave us or forsake us—ever. The only way we as believers can be separated from God is if we turn our backs and walk away from Him. The enemy will do all he can to discourage us. He will tell us God is angry with us and has turned away from us just to get us to turn our backs on God. These two men chose not to let their circumstances cause them to reject God. Ultimately God exalted and vindicated both of them after they had walked through some very trying circumstances.

We will find ourselves in times where God doesn't seem to be there or responding, but we must remember that He is there, and He will respond. We must stand on His promise that He will never leave or forsake us and not turn away from Him. These men remained faithful, and God was faithful with them. Neither tried to defend themselves. Instead, they accepted the rulings and the punishments, and yet they eventually found favor in each circumstance.

I would like to think I could do that, as well, but I could not possibly do it if I thought God had abandoned me. I have been falsely accused a couple of times in my career. In the first instance, I did not respond well. Why? Because I made it about me. I was more concerned about justifying myself than I was about keeping my eye on the overall objective. I didn't fully trust God in the situation.

Joseph and Daniel trusted God, and each was delivered from some very dark and dangerous circumstances, and they both were restored to positions of even greater authority. Why? Because they were faithful, they possessed the wisdom of God, and they brought that to bear for the kings' benefit. The stories end with both being honored by kings and given positions of greater influence in the kingdom.

For Joseph:

> *And Pharaoh said to his servants, Can we find this man's equal, a man in whom is the spirit of God? And Pharaoh said to Joseph, Forasmuch as [your] God has shown you all this, there is nobody as intelligent and discreet and understanding and wise as you are. You shall have charge over my house, and all my people shall be governed according to your word [with reverence, submission, and obedience]. Only in matters of the throne will I be greater than you are.*
>
>

Genesis 41:38–40 (AMP)

> *But when all the land of Egypt was weakened with hunger, the people [there] cried to Pharaoh for food; and Pharaoh said to [them] all, Go to Joseph; what he says to you, do. When the famine was over all the land, Joseph opened all the storehouses and sold to the Egyptians; for the famine grew extremely distressing in the land of Egypt. And all countries came to Egypt to Joseph to buy grain, because the famine was severe over all [the known] earth.*
>
>

Genesis 41:55–57 (AMP)

For Daniel:

> *Then King Darius wrote to all peoples, nations, and languages [in his realm] that dwelt in all the earth:*

May peace be multiplied to you! I make a decree that in all my royal dominion men must tremble and fear before the God of Daniel, for He is the living God, enduring and steadfast forever, and His kingdom shall not be destroyed and His dominion shall be even to the end [of the world]. He is a Savior and Deliverer, and He works signs and wonders in the heavens and on the earth—He Who has delivered Daniel from the power of the lions. So this [man] Daniel prospered in the reign of Darius and in the reign of Cyrus the Persian.

Daniel 6:25–28 (AMP)

What a lesson for us. There may come a time when we have reached a level of influence that impacts many people. We are blessed, and we know God has put us there. Then out of nowhere, we are wrongly accused, and it all seems to fall apart through no fault of our own.

The Bible says we will face tribulation, so what will we do then? Will we still maintain our integrity, our love for God, and our love for others? These two men did, and they were then able to use their restored positions of influence to ease the suffering of many and help their kings prosper. God positioned them so they could alleviate pain and suffering in entire regions of the world.

The stories of Joseph and Daniel are two powerful accounts of men being faithful to God and God being faithful to His promises. But maybe, even more importantly, the leaders of the day recognized both as being led by a God the leaders did not know. Joseph and Daniel possessed a wisdom and understanding that surpassed all the other counselors of the day. It was their witness, their ministry, and God received glory from the kings for it. The Bible tells us the very same wisdom is available to us as followers of Christ.

It is easy to think of these accounts as just stories or fables and forget that Joseph and Daniel were two real people, just like you and me, who faced tremendous challenges yet did not bow to the pressure and compromise their integrity. Each account provides a consistent approach to handling the attacks of the enemy that will come with each promotion you receive.

I have heard Joyce Meyer say, "new level, new devil." I believe that to be true. As our influence increases, so does the enemy's desire to destroy that influence, and as I said before, the more influence you have, the bigger impact you can have, both positively and negatively. How will we use it? To help and serve others or to magnify ourselves? It is one or the other—a binary decision. There is no middle ground.

We may never (and I hope I don't) face situations as difficult as Joseph and Daniel, but we will have our integrity and our faithfulness challenged multiple times in our lives. Jesus said persecution will follow God's blessings. As a follower of Christ, you will encounter times when the pressure seems so great that you don't know if you will be able to get beyond it. When that happens, I can guarantee the enemy will be right there telling you that you weren't treated fairly, and everyone would understand if you compromised just this one time to relieve the pressure because everyone else does it. He'll be saying, "You can give in to this temptation to tell someone off or to lie just this once because others do it."

Don't do it! Resist it! Just as God did for Daniel and Joseph, He will see you through to victory in those situations. He has promised that if we remain faithful, He has our backs, and He will show out for us in those situations. He will see you through to the other side of the tribulation. Why? Because just as it was for Joseph and Daniel once they were restored, there are many who require the blessings you are uniquely positioned to provide.

As these accounts show, God desires His people to be in positions of influence so they can have a positive impact on the communities around them. It is also clear from Scripture that God has a role for His people in business, and it is His desire for them to succeed in that role. His measure of success is different than what is taught in business schools, however, because it is based on how effectively we use our gifts and influence to serve and love others—to be salt and light in the world.

Displaying His nature to the world is true witnessing. We will spend the rest of this book exploring how to apply biblical principles to minister to (serve) our colleagues, our businesses, and our communities in our roles in the marketplace, giving God all the glory as we do it.

Business as a Calling | Derick Masengale

SECTION TWO

Spiritual Fundamentals

CHAPTER 3

The Kingdom of God Is As If...

And He said, with what can we compare the kingdom of God, or what parable shall we use to illustrate and explain it? It is like a grain of mustard seed, which, when sown upon the ground, is the smallest of all seeds upon the earth; Yet after it is sown, it grows up and becomes the greatest of all garden herbs and puts out large branches, so that the birds of the air are able to make nests and dwell in its shade.

Mark 4:30–32 (AMP)

In the previous section, we discussed the place of work and business in our personal lives, and I presented a perspective of how we can use our roles in the marketplace to minister to others and further God's kingdom. As a reminder, Genesis 1:28 (AMP) states:

And God blessed them and said to them, Be fruitful, multiply, and fill the earth, and subdue it [using all its vast resources in the service of God and man]; and have dominion over the fish of the sea, the birds of the air, and over every living creature that moves upon the earth.

God gave Adam and Eve a job to do and blessed them by fully equipping them (gifting them) to accomplish His Word. The command was and still is to increase and use the resources God provides to produce results that bless God and man, and we discussed the role of business in fulfilling that command: (1) by providing goods and services to a community to help it flourish, and (2) by providing opportunities for individuals to use and grow their God-given talents and gifts to produce those goods and services. God gave man dominion over all the earth to accomplish His command, but when Adam and Eve sinned, they gave that dominion over to the enemy. Genesis 3:17 (AMP) says:

> And to Adam He said, Because you have listened and given heed to the voice of your wife and have eaten of the tree of which I commanded you, saying, You shall not eat of it, the ground is under a curse because of you; in sorrow and toil shall you eat [of the fruits] of it all the days of your life.

This verse tells us that as a result of that sinful act, man now has to toil to subdue the earth—he no longer has dominion over all that was in the earth because he gave it to Satan. As a result, work became much more difficult. Why? Because man is now separated from God. He no longer has God's grace to do the work commanded of him. His work now becomes toil. Man no longer works to fulfill God's command; he is now working to provide food and shelter for himself.

This is a fundamental principle to grasp. God did not intend us to work to provide for ourselves. He intended us to work in the service of God and man to grow His kingdom. God tells us many times in His Word that He is our provider, not our vocation, and we need not worry about what we are to eat or drink or what clothes we will wear. He will use our positions to provide resources to meet our needs and give us financial seeds to sow (more on this later), but that is not His only way.

So much of the bad behavior we see in the business world is a result of people striving to provide or get for themselves. Often being driven by the fear of not having enough, they are toiling. This is not a criticism; it is an observation, and it is understandable behavior based on the training most people get. However, if we add biblically-based spiritual training to our educational training, we will have a different perspective.

You might say, "The Word said man would now have to toil to get the ground to produce, and I feel I am toiling at my work." Yes, it does, but the good news is because of Jesus' sacrifice at the cross, we are no longer separated from God and under the curse. He makes Himself available again through His Word and His Holy Spirit so that we now have dominion again over all the earth.

This means the toil aspect of work can be removed, and we can find joy in our work once again by performing it in the service of God and man as God originally intended. We can do that by knowing that God declared in His Word that He is our provider, and it is His will for us, as His children, to succeed in all that we do. So how do we get better aligned with God and the Holy Spirit so that our work can be fulfilling to us and be a blessing to others?

It starts by recognizing that the primary way God speaks to us is through the written words in the Bible. Before making the decision to follow Jesus, I had read the Bible and even took a New Testament course in college, which required me to study the Bible. The course was centered on the historical Jesus, not on the spiritual aspects of the Gospel. So it never dawned on me that God wanted to talk to me through the Bible. I viewed it as more of a religious book full of rules and the New Testament Gospels as historical accounts of Jesus' time on earth.

To this day, I remember the professor beginning the class by saying, "We will be studying the historical Jesus; however, I hope this course will also help you grow spiritually." I thought that was odd, and it wasn't until years later that I actually understood what he said. Looking at the Bible as God's Word to me was not a concept I had heard in the churches I attended growing up and, frankly, not one I had even considered.

It wasn't until I became desperate enough to ask God to show me if He and the Bible were real that I got a revelation on the importance of God's written Word. It wasn't until I started to view what was written through a faith lens and not through a religious lens that I became excited about what was written in the pages of the Bible. It wasn't until I accepted Jesus as my Lord and Savior that the Holy Spirit came to provide confirmation and revelation of God's Word to me. In a short period of time, I realized the Bible was not a book of rules that restricts life, but in fact, it is a book of promises that expands life. Religion restricts life; knowledge of and faith in the promises of God's Word expands life. That revelation changed my outlook on life forever.

> *I realized that it was not a book of rules that restricts life but in fact, it is a book of promises that expands life.*

If you are unsure of the relevance of God's Word, I challenge you to test it for yourself. If you truly want to know if God and His Word are real and alive, pray the simple prayer that I prayed and ask Him to show you that He is real and that His Word is real. Once you've done that, you can't just sit and wait for something to fall from heaven. You must do your part: seek Him. I would suggest you spend at least one hour a day reading the Word and praying. Do it consistently for thirty days. If you seek God, He will show up. His Word declares it, and it also declares that He is no respecter of persons. What He has done for others, He will do for you. He will reveal Himself to anyone who is searching. If you accept the challenge, I am certain you will have a different view of the Bible and God by the end of those thirty days. You may say, "It's a big book. I don't know where to start." I would suggest starting with the book of Proverbs and the Gospel of John.

I had heard the message that we were all sinners many times. I was raised in a denomination that focused on that concept, and I knew I was a sinner, but I didn't know what to do about it. No matter how hard I tried to get all the sin out of my life, I could not do it. I was not taught the message of grace (I have dedicated an entire chapter in this book to the concept of grace) and the freedom that comes with it. Once I got hold of that message, it changed everything for me. I began to read and study the Word with great expectations. I found throughout the Word that it was God's desire for us to increase and be blessed. Deuteronomy 8:11–18 (ASV) says:

> *Beware lest thou forget Jehovah thy God, in not keeping his commandments, and his ordinances, and his statutes, which I command thee this day: lest, when thou hast eaten and art full, and hast built goodly houses, and dwelt therein; and when thy herds and thy flocks multiply, and thy silver and thy gold is multiplied, and all that thou hast is multiplied; then thy*

*heart be lifted up, and thou forget Jehovah thy God,
who brought thee forth out of the land of Egypt, out of
the house of bondage; who led thee through the great
and terrible wilderness, wherein were fiery serpents
and scorpions, and thirsty ground where was no water;
who brought thee forth water out of the rock of flint;
who fed thee in the wilderness with manna, which thy
fathers knew not; that he might humble thee, and that
he might prove thee, to do thee good at thy latter end:
and lest thou say in thy heart, My power and the might
of my hand hath gotten me this wealth. But thou shalt
remember Jehovah thy God, for it is he that giveth thee
power to get wealth; that he may establish his covenant
which he sware unto thy fathers, as at this day.*

This passage is a description of a prosperous people, but it also puts prosperity into context. We are to humble ourselves and honor God. We are to recognize that He has given us the power to get wealth, and He tells us why—to establish His covenant. It is God's will for us to be blessed with good homes and wealth, but He wants us to use some of our resources to establish His covenant. He gives us power to get wealth, but He wants us to use our wealth to bless others, not just ourselves. That does not mean only our financial wealth. You may have a wealth of knowledge you can share, or you may have a wealth of experience and wisdom to share. All these can be used to bless others. Without God, we are relying on our own power and understanding; we are toiling. This explains why I was struggling in school and running my business before connecting with God.

He tells us in 3 John 1:2 that we prosper even as our soul prospers. It was a tremendously exciting thing for me to learn that

God wanted me to prosper and that I *should* expect to prosper if I follow Him. I wanted to prosper. I was tired of toiling, of failing, and of living in lack. As I mentioned, I tried a lot of things only to be disappointed with the outcomes of each. I'm a bottom-line guy. If something I'm doing doesn't produce positive results, I'm ready to move on to the next option. I wanted results, and God was gracious and allowed me to see those results. And that made me hungry for more.

In the beginning, I can't say my motives were all that pure. I just wanted to overcome lack, but God worked with me as I sought Him to help me recognize that His prosperity wasn't just about making me more comfortable. Over time, He helped me focus on people other than myself. God is a loving God; He meets you where you are. You don't have to get everything "under control" before you reach out to Him. He will help you grow and mature as you continue to seek Him.

Admittedly, I was probably more willing to believe that God blesses His children more than others just because my life had spiraled so low, and I needed to believe in something. Everything I tried had failed, so I was looking for a new and better way. However, I recognize that people who do not know Jesus can make good decisions and use a strong work ethic to achieve a level of success in the world and believe it was completely based on their education, skill, and hard work. They are deceived—no exceptions. I know that is a bold statement; however, no one achieves success on their own. Whether they admit it or not, they relied on the work and contributions of many others—family, teachers, professors, co-workers, coaches, mentors, etc.—to achieve their success. God may have influenced some of these people to help you succeed.

Sadly, we have all heard many stories of individuals who have succeeded greatly in an area of life, but once they achieved that success, they asked themselves, "Is this all there is? Am I just working to get more stuff and to make a name for myself? When will I be satisfied?" They could not tie their success to a greater purpose. Looking into God's Word and understanding how He defines success will bring that insight. It will lead you to true satisfaction, which will require dependence on God.

If our vision is just seeing our success and reaching some position of perceived importance, we will never be satisfied. We will get to that position and realize we are still not the most important person in the room, company, city, etc. and we'll keep striving for the next title or milestone. God's will is for us to prosper with a purpose, and that purpose is greater than meeting the needs and desires of just us or our families: it is to establish His kingdom. We can learn what our purpose is only by spending time with God in prayer and reading His Word.

So, if it is God's will for us to prosper in business, then how do we do that according to His plan, and how do we prosper with a God-given purpose? As I said previously, we need to seek God to understand where He is calling us. We need to listen for God's direction and then measure what we sense or think against the Word of God. *The primary way God speaks to us is through His Word, the Bible.* Everything we hear and the decisions we make must be measured against the Word of God. The better we get at aligning our decisions with the Word of God, the more success we will experience. We can also be sure that God is *never* going to ask us to do something that is not aligned with the direction provided in His Word. If we hear (have thoughts about) something that is not aligned with the Word of God, it is not God talking to us, no exceptions.

Okay, you may be saying, "I am intrigued. How do I study the Word, hear from God, and put it into practice? It is a big book. Where and how do I start?" Let's start by looking at what Jesus describes as the fundamental principle of how the kingdom of God operates. It is found in Mark 4:1–12 (KJV):

> *And he began again to teach by the sea side: and there was gathered unto him a great multitude, so that he entered into a ship, and sat in the sea; and the whole multitude was by the sea on the land. And he taught them many things by parables, and said unto them in his doctrine, Hearken; Behold, there went out a sower to sow: And it came to pass, as he sowed, some fell by the way side, and the fowls of the air came and devoured it up. And some fell on stony ground, where it had not much earth; and immediately it sprang up, because it had no depth of earth: But when the sun was up, it was scorched; and because it had no root, it withered away. And some fell among thorns, and the thorns grew up, and choked it, and it yielded no fruit. And other fell on good ground, and did yield fruit that sprang up and increased; and brought forth, some thirty, and some sixty, and some an hundred. And he said unto them, He that hath ears to hear, let him hear. And when he was alone, they that were about him with the twelve asked of him the parable. And he said unto them, Unto you it is given to know the mystery of the kingdom of God: but unto them that are without, all these things are done in parables: That seeing they may see, and not perceive; and hearing they may hear,*

and not understand; lest at any time they should be converted, and their sins should be forgiven them.

Jesus said in verse 11, "unto you it is given to know the mystery of the kingdom of God." The "you" in this scrip-

> *The primary way God speaks to us is through His Word—the Bible.*

ture refers to anyone who has accepted Jesus as their Lord and Savior. How are the insight and understanding given? Through the study of His Word and by the presence and witness of His Holy Spirit. By His Spirit speaking to ours, we can know the mysteries. We will discuss this in more detail in a subsequent chapter.

When I was taking the New Testament class I mentioned earlier, I was studying the Bible, I was doing it as an academic exercise. I needed to learn the material so I could take a test. It was a soulish exercise—it was done completely with my mind. I needed to read and memorize the accounts in the Bible. I did not ask God for help understanding what was written. I was viewing it as a historical study and approaching it as I would any other academic subject. Frankly, I didn't even think I could ask God for help understanding the text, and even if I did, I didn't know how to hear His voice, so I wouldn't have known if He was speaking to me. As a result, I got very little out of the study other than some knowledge of the events that took place in Jesus' life. I was among the group of people referenced in verse 12 who could see and not perceive.

A couple of years later, when I asked God to show me if the Bible was real, I unknowingly authorized the Holy Spirit to provide revelation of the Word to me. I didn't realize I had made that request of the Holy Spirit until later, and I didn't understand what the Holy Spirit's role was in confirming the Word and the will of God until much later. But I knew something had changed. The experience of reading and studying the Word was completely different. Something inside me was different. I recognized truth in the Word, and I found encouragement; I saw promises. The Holy Spirit was at work in me. I had a knowing deep inside that was confirming amazing things I was finding in Scripture. At the same time, I received some excellent teaching on this topic, and I saw in Scripture that I could use the Word to change and improve my life. Continuing with verse 13:

And he said unto them, Know ye not this parable? and how then will ye know all parables? The sower soweth the word. And these are they by the way side, where the word is sown; but when they have heard, Satan cometh immediately, and taketh away the word that was sown in their hearts. And these are they likewise which are sown on stony ground; who, when they have heard the word, immediately receive it with gladness; And have no root in themselves, and so endure but for a time: afterward, when affliction or persecution ariseth for the word's sake, immediately they are offended. And these are they which are sown among thorns; such as hear the word, And the cares of this world, and the deceitful-ness of riches, and the lusts of other things entering in, choke the word, and it becometh unfruitful. And these are they which are sown on good ground; such as hear the word, and receive it, and bring forth fruit, some thirtyfold, some sixty, and some an hundred. And he said unto them, Is a candle brought to be put under a bushel, or under a bed? and not to be set on a candle-

*stick? For there is nothing hid, which shall not be man-
ifested; neither was any thing kept secret, but that it
should come abroad. If any man have ears to hear, let
him hear. And he said unto them, Take heed what ye
hear: with what measure ye mete, it shall be measured
to you: and unto you that hear shall more be given.*

These scriptures describe how the Word of God produces results in our lives. It provides a clear picture of how to apply the Word, prompted by the Holy Spirit, and great insight on what we are to watch for to protect the seed (the Word) that is sown. These scriptures tell me I can "sow" (speak) the Word and expect it to produce results in my life. If I am ignorant of the promises in the Word of God, then I have no seed to sow to produce an outcome in my life that aligns with God's promises. This teaching opened my eyes to how the kingdom of God operates and why it is important to study the Word. How important is the Word of God?

> *"Therefore My people go into exile for want of knowl-
> edge; their honored men are dying of hunger, and their
> multitude is parched with thirst."*

> Isaiah 5:13 (The New Oxford Annotated Bible)

> *"My people are destroyed for lack of knowledge; because
> you [the priestly nation] have rejected knowledge, I will
> also reject you that you shall be no priest to Me; seeing
> you have forgotten the law of your God, I will also
> forget your children."*

> Hosea 4:6 (AMP)

God says His people can be led into captivity and be destroyed by a lack of knowledge of His Word. Believers in God and His Son can go into exile. All of us have seen many examples of individuals not being aware of what is in God's Word or being aware and rejecting the guidance only to head down the path of pain and destruction—divorce, drug and alcohol addiction, broken relationships, and greed. Worse yet, they may feel alone in their agony and believe no one cares for them. They do not know God loves them and has a good plan for their lives. Without the knowledge of the Word, it is impossible to know what God's will is. The New Testament is called the good news for a reason. The Bible is a book of promises from God to us. What measure do we want to mete? What will we believe? One of the most impactful verses in the Bible for me is Mark 4:24 (AMP): "And He said to them, be careful what you are hearing. The measure [of thought and study] you give [to the truth you hear] will be the measure [of virtue and knowledge] that comes back to you—and more [besides] will be given to you who hear."

How do I get a thirty-, sixty-, or hundred-fold return on the Word I have sown by confessing His promises? The measure of thought and study I give to the truth I hear is the measure of what comes back to me. We alone, not God, determine the power of the Word in our lives. That may not align with your religious teaching, but it is God's Word to us. The Bible tells us we decide what we hear and guard in our hearts. I remind myself of this verse regularly. When the enemy tries to convince me the obstacle I am facing is too big, I just remind myself it is the measure *I mete* that determines the return on the Word I sow, not the circumstances I am facing.

I realize this may sound simplistic to some, and to others, it may sound like some form of positive thinking, but it is much more than that. It is knowing what God says about a situation and choosing to stand on the promise even when all hell is breaking loose around me. We choose what we believe, God's promises or the circumstances swirling around us. No one can make us believe anything, and we can't believe both of them at the same time. Which will you choose?

The following verses in Mark 4 (AMP) describe the kingdom of God:

> *And He said, with what can we compare the kingdom of God, or what parable shall we use to illustrate and explain it? It is like a grain of mustard seed, which, when sown upon the ground, is the smallest of all seeds upon the earth; Yet after it is sown, it grows up and becomes the greatest of all garden herbs and puts out large branches, so that the birds of the air are able to make nests and dwell in its shade.*

We saw in the earlier verses that Jesus said the Word of God is a seed, and these verses tell us the kingdom of God operates based on a seed that is sown into the ground; it grows, produces fruit, and is harvested. How does this model apply to our daily work activities? How do we apply it daily in our calling in the business world? We can start by looking at how seeds are sown.

Words are our seeds. What we say determines our eventual outcome, good or bad. This is true whether you believe it or not. We intuitively know this, and most people would much rather associate with someone who is positive and encouraging in their conversations than someone who is always negative. We need to check ourselves to see whether we are speaking words that align with God's promises or whether we are sowing words that contradict what the Word of God says about a given situation. Jesus provides insight on how to produce results by sowing the Word in Mark 4:15–20 (AMP):

> *The ones along the path are those who have the Word sown [in their hearts], but when they hear, Satan comes at once and [by force] takes away the message which is sown in them. And in the same way the ones sown upon stony ground are those who, when they hear the Word, at once receive and accept and welcome it with joy; And they have no real root in themselves, and so they endure for a little while; then when trouble or persecution arises on account of the Word, they immediately are offended (become displeased, indignant, resentful) and they stumble and fall away. And the ones sown among the thorns are others who hear the Word; Then the cares and anxieties of the world and distractions of the age, and the pleasure and delight and false glamour and deceitfulness of riches, and the craving and passionate desire for other things creep in and choke and suffocate the Word, and it becomes fruitless. And those sown on the good (well-adapted) soil are the ones who hear the Word and receive and accept and welcome it and bear fruit—some thirty times as much as was sown, some sixty times as much, and some [even] a hundred times as much.*

To produce the thirty-, sixty-, or one-hundred-fold harvest, we need to sow (speak) the Word and then tend to the Word sown in our hearts to keep our faith strong and stand on the promises from the Word we sowed. As the scripture above says, we need to tend it to prevent the enemy from destroying our crop (our desired result). Jesus said in John 10:10 (AMP), "The thief comes only in order to steal and kill and destroy. I came that they may have *and* enjoy life, and have it in abundance (to the full, till it overflows)." The enemy is trying to first steal the seed (prevent you from hearing and sowing the Word), and if that doesn't work, he is trying to kill the crop before you harvest your thirty-, sixty-, or one-hundred-fold harvest. How does he do it? Jesus tells us in verses 17, 18, and 19 that it is primarily through:

- Affliction
- Persecution
- Cares of the world
- Deceitfulness of riches
- Lust for other things

These are Satan's tools for choking off the Word once it is sown. While we are standing in faith in God's promises, Satan will come at us with these ploys to get us to dig up our own crop. How does that happen? By allowing the pressure and fear caused by these tactics to get us off God's promises and begin to confess an outcome that is different from what is promised in the Word, one that is based on the circumstances we are facing. Our recognition of these tactics and how to shut them down is key to us receiving God's promises. Resisting these forms of attack is tough enough when we are aware they are coming and why. It is impossible when we are ignorant of the tactics. Below are examples of how these manifest in our daily lives:

- Affliction (physical): we can work so hard and toil for so long that we weaken our body and create an open door for sickness to enter in. Once this occurs, we can blame God and ask why He hasn't healed us and why He let it happen. At some point, He probably told us to rest, and we ignored the suggestion. Once this happens, our focus is turned toward a physical ailment and off the promises we believe will come to pass.

- Persecution: if we operate in God's integrity and blessing, some may become jealous, while others may tell us how foolish we are to believe God for anything. We saw that in the lives of Joseph and Daniel. Influential people may ridicule us for taking a stand on how we operate and how we treat our co-workers and business partners. Will we allow that to change our confession and actions?

- Cares of this world: "I know what God's Word says, but I need to look out for number one. If I don't watch out for myself, then no one else will. If I don't, I might not get the position or raise I want." Or we let the current economic conditions convince us that what God says about prospering us must not be correct because He cannot possibly prosper anyone in the current economic climate.

- Deceitfulness of riches: "The more money I have, the happier I will be and the more good I can do. I plan to do good when I become rich, no matter how I get there. The ends will justify the means. It is the riches that will make me happy, not how I can bless others with my influence and financial resources."

- Lust for other things: working for things for ourselves without having a vision for why God is prospering us. We are just continuing to focus on getting more. This does not necessarily mean only material things; we could be lusting for a position with more power.

Over the years, I have found the enemy comes at me most with the cares of this world. It is not always obvious; it can sneak up on me. There is a fine line between being responsible for what is in my control and allowing the cares about those things I can't control to come in and choke the Word. It is my obligation to meet the responsibilities regarding the things I can control. For the many things that are not in my control, however, I can believe God will honor the promises in His Word, or I can believe the lies the enemy is telling me about how irresponsible I am because I am trusting God, and I need to get myself or others to do more.

This can lead to all sorts of bad behaviors. For example, I may not delegate responsibilities as effectively as I should because I am afraid that someone can't perform the task as well as I can. Or Satan will try to get me to act in haste by telling me if I don't do something immediately, I am being irresponsible, and disaster will occur. In those situations, he is trying to get me to act out of fear and not faith. I know I am in good company in that regard. Mark 4:35–40 (AMP) provides an amazing account of what happens later that day after Jesus had taught on the sowing and reaping principle:

> *On that same day [when] evening had come, He said to them, Let us go over to the other side [of the lake]. And leaving the throng, they took Him with*

them, [just] as He was, in the boat [in which He was
sitting]. And other boats were with Him. And a furious
storm of wind [of hurricane proportions] arose, and
the waves kept beating into the boat, so that it was
already becoming filled. But He [Himself] was in the
stern [of the boat], asleep on the [leather] cushion;
and they awoke Him and said to Him, Master, do
You not care that we are perishing? And He arose and
rebuked the wind and said to the sea, Hush now! Be
still (muzzled)! And the wind ceased (sank to rest as if
exhausted by its beating) and there was [immediately]
a great calm (a perfect peacefulness). He said to them,
Why are you so timid and fearful? How is it that you
have no faith (no firmly relying trust)?

Jesus had been sowing the Word all day into the apostles and the multitudes. Then, when He was alone with the apostles, He took even more time to explain in detail what the parables meant and how fundamental they are to operating in the kingdom of God. Finally, after many hours of teaching, He told the apostles to get in the boat and go to the other side. They got in, and Jesus went to sleep. While in the boat, a great storm came, and they were afraid. While Jesus was asleep in the boat, the enemy immediately used the cares of this world to steal the Word that was sown into the apostles.

A big storm arose, and the apostles began to fear for their lives. Amongst all the turmoil, the apostles woke Jesus and said, "Carest thou not that we perish?" He then used His words to calm the storm. If all of them had drowned, that certainly would have prevented the seed Jesus had been sowing all day from producing in the apostles' lives. What would that have done to the future of the church? Those men became the early church leaders, and Satan came immediately to steal, kill, and destroy the seeds sown, and they were complicit via their own confessions. The apostles' words were, "we are going to die." Jesus' words were "peace be still," and the seas obeyed. The sea didn't obey because it was Jesus; it obeyed because Jesus spoke the words of God.

Later in His ministry, He told the apostles that He speaks only what the Father tells Him to speak, and He does only what the Father tells Him to do. In this case, the Father told Him to go to the other side and rest on the way over. When He awoke, His direction and goal were the same, go to the other side. So, He spoke to the situation to make it conform to what God had spoken to Him. We as believers have the same authority to speak God's will into existence in any situation by speaking His anointed words as prompted by the Holy Spirit. Are we prepared to believe that? Will we continue to confess it when it seems all hell is breaking loose against us?

What words do you hear yourself say when you are under great pressure? Are they words of fear or words based on God's promises? Just as the enemy did with the apostles, he will try to make the Word we hear unfruitful. We must not forget that the enemy will try to steal the Word when we sow it. We must guard our hearts by choosing what we hear and use our faith to stand on God's promises. One final thought to consider. Both Hebrews and Ephesians refer to the Word as the sword of the Spirit.

> *For the Word that God speaks is alive and full of power*
> *[making it active, operative, energizing, and effective];*
> *it is sharper than any two-edged sword, penetrating to*
> *the dividing line of the breath of life (soul) and [the*
> *immortal] spirit, and of joints and marrow [of the*

deepest parts of our nature], exposing and sifting and
analyzing and judging the very thoughts and purposes
of the heart.

Hebrews 4:12 (AMP)

And take the helmet of salvation and the sword that
the Spirit wields, which is the Word of God.

Ephesians 6:17 (AMP)

God has provided us armor to protect us from the attack of the enemy, but most importantly, He has provided us one offensive weapon: the Word of God. It is up to us to know the Word, to speak it, and to act on it to bring God's will to pass in our lives, our workplaces, and our communities. The Word is spiritual, and if we want to bring it to bear in our professions, we must bring our spiritual self to work. We will talk about this later, but the Word is the offensive weapon that God provides for us to combat the wiles of the devil.

However, not every situation we encounter is directly covered in the Bible. For example:

- What investments should I make?
- I have three candidates for a role; whom should I pick?
- I have conflicting reports; which one is true?

So, what do you do when you can't find a specific answer in the Word? How do you know God's will for that situation? The Bible tells us that God has made a way. He sent His Holy Spirit to guide us in all things. John 14:26 (AMP) states:

But the Comforter (Counselor, Helper, Intercessor,
Advocate, Strengthener, Standby), the Holy Spirit,
Whom the Father will send in My name [in My place,
to represent Me and act on My behalf], He will teach
you all things. And He will cause you to recall (will
remind you of, bring to your remembrance) everything
I have told you.

In the next chapter, we will learn the role the Holy Spirit plays in providing God's guidance for the decisions we need to make each day.

CHAPTER 4

Person and Purpose of the Holy Spirit

But when He, the Spirit of Truth (the Truth-giving Spirit) comes, He will guide you into all the Truth (the whole, full Truth). For He will not speak His own message [on His own authority]; but He will tell whatever He hears [from the Father; He will give the message that has been given to Him], and He will announce and declare to you the things that are to come [that will happen in the future].

John 16:13 (AMP)

I want to start this chapter by reiterating that God speaks to everyone who seeks Him for insight, and the number one way He speaks to us is through His Word. Matthew 4:4 (AMP) says, "It has been written, Man shall not live *and* be upheld *and* sustained by bread alone, but by every word that comes forth from the mouth of God." It is on us to study His Word to know His will and promises for us. As we learned, we must speak and act on His Word as we encounter circumstances that try to prevent His promises from coming to pass in our lives. The Word provides clear direction for many of the personal and business decisions we must make. But what do you do when you need to make a decision that is not specifically covered in the Word?

For example, does God care about where you live, who you marry, or what job you take? Does He care about your business decisions or who you hire? Does He care about whether you pursue this business opportunity or whether this is the right business partner? It is clear from the Word that He does, and it is clear from His Word that He wants us to seek His guidance in all that we do, not so He can control us, but so He can position us for success. First Peter 5:7 (AMP) says: "Casting the whole of your care [all your anxieties, all your worries, all your concerns, once and for all] on Him, for He cares for you affectionately and cares about you watchfully."

And Psalm 8:4 (AMP) says: "What is man that You are mindful of him, and the son of [earthborn] man that You care for him?"

God has told us to cast the whole (or all) of our cares (including those related to the workplace) unto Him because He cares for us. He is our Father. He wants to see us happy and satisfied. Just as you would give your children help if they asked, He desires to give each of us the insight and help to know how to make the daily decisions I just described.

We can find guidance in the Word of God to help us answer those questions, but we can't find specific answers. The good news is that God has given us what we need to guide us through these types of situations.

Four or five years after I made the decision to base my life on following the Lord, I was on a business trip and in a hotel room in Houston, Texas. Up until that time, I had been focused on studying the Word and building my faith by hearing and sowing the Word, as we discussed in the previous chapter. I was in Houston to test launch software I had written in the Space Shuttle Avionics and Instrumentation Lab at the Johnson Space

Center. At that time, when engineers from the Kennedy Space Center went to the lab at the Johnson Space Center to test, we could only get time in the testing facility on the third shift (from 11 p.m. to 7 a.m.). Because of the drastic change in my work schedule, when I went there, I didn't really sleep much. It was too difficult to adjust my sleeping schedule in the middle of a week and sleep more than three or four hours at a time.

I was lying in the hotel bed one afternoon, reading the Bible and praying, and I said to God, "I understand You've given us Your Word, and we are to sow it and believe it, but I think there is more to this, and I need to know what it is. Please show me." Within a couple of hours, one of the folks who was on the trip with me knocked on my door and said, "Hey, Benny Hinn is in town." She attended his church in Orlando at the time. "Hal and I are going to his service tonight. Do you want to come?"

I said, "Sure."

So, we went to the Compaq Center, which is now where Joel Osteen's Lakewood Church meets, to attend the service.

That night God answered the prayer I had prayed that afternoon (I wish I could always get answers to my prayers that fast!). During the service, my eyes were opened to the ministry of the Holy Spirit. I didn't understand everything that was going on during the service, and some of it seemed strange, but I understood that God answered my prayer and that His power flowed through the ministry of the Holy Spirit. From that point on, I have sought to learn as much as I can about the Holy Spirit and all that God makes available to us through Him.

Having said that, let's investigate Scripture so we can begin to understand who the Holy Spirit is, why it is important to be led by Him, and how we can allow Him to lead us in our daily walk with God. This includes our time spent working in our professions. First, let's start by getting an understanding of who the Holy Spirit is. In John 16:12–15 (AMP), Jesus tells us much about the Holy Spirit:

> *I have still many things to say to you, but you are not able to bear them or to take them upon you or to grasp them now. But when He, the Spirit of Truth (the Truth-giving Spirit) comes, He will guide you into all the Truth (the whole, full Truth). For He will not speak His own message [on His own authority]; but He will tell whatever He hears [from the Father; He will give the message that has been given to Him], and He will announce and declare to you the things that are to come [that will happen in the future]. He will honor and glorify Me, because He will take of (receive, draw upon) what is Mine and will reveal (declare, disclose, transmit) it to you. Everything that the Father has is Mine. That is what I meant when I said that He [the Spirit] will take the things that are Mine and will reveal (declare, disclose, transmit) it to you.*

One thing made clear in this passage is that the Holy Spirit is a person and not an "it." This is a very important concept that we must have settled in our minds if we want the Holy Spirit to guide us. The word "it" refers to an inanimate object and not a person. We never refer to a person as an "it," but we do refer to things as "it." For example, I just got a new car; "it" is really nice. "Derick, that is kind of silly. Why does this matter?" you ask. It matters for this reason: you can't have a relationship with an inanimate object. You may talk to that thing and have an emotional attachment to it, but that thing is never going to return the conversation. Looking at this passage of Scripture, we see that Jesus refers to the Holy Spirit using personal pronouns—thirteen times in fact. From Jesus' teaching in this passage, it is clear that the Holy Spirit is a person, and God sent Him to speak to us.

Scripture says the Holy Spirit has been sent to have a relationship with us, and Jesus specifies what type of relationship it is:

- He will guide us into all truth. Do you ever find yourself in a situation where you have conflicting information and you are trying to figure out what is correct? According to Jesus, the Holy Spirit knows and will guide us in determining what is true.

- He will tell us whatever He hears the Father say, and He will announce things that are to come. Do you want to know what decision to make to stay in God's will in a situation? Do you want to know things to come? This scripture tells us that God sent the Holy Spirit to provide that insight.

However, just because the Holy Spirit is speaking to us, that does not mean we are listening. Just as in any relationship, if you want to develop it, you must spend time with that person. Similarly, we must spend time with the Holy Spirit to develop

Revelation from the Word comes from the outside in, while revelation from the Holy Spirit starts from the inside out.

a relationship with Him so we can learn His nature and know how to communicate with Him. In the previous chapter, we talked about obtaining revelation from God through studying the Word and applying it to our lives. In this chapter, we are talking about receiving revelation from God through the Holy Spirit and applying it to our lives. We must take that guidance from the Holy Spirit by faith. As we will learn, He is constantly talking to us and sharing God's plan for us. We must make it a priority to develop the relationship so we know how to differentiate a thought prompted by the Holy Spirit from other thoughts we may have rolling around in our mind.

It is important to recognize and consider that revelation from the Word starts from the outside in, while revelation from the Holy Spirit starts from the inside out. When I read or hear the Word of God, it moves through my mind (soul) and has to get into my spirit. We have discussed how Satan comes to steal the Word before it gets to our spirit. However, revelation from our spirit starts from the inside out. God's Holy Spirit speaks to our spirit, and the revelation must move from our spirit to our mind (soul). The cares of this world can continue to spin through my mind, impacting my ability to "hear" what my spirit is saying, but God is still speaking. Just as the enemy is continually trying to steal the Word to prevent God's promises from coming to pass, the enemy is continually trying to convince us that we can't or didn't hear from God via the Holy Spirit to know God's will in a given situation.

God uses both channels to teach us about Him and His will for us. Are we taking advantage of both of these channels? I have learned that if I am going to be effective in all areas of my life, I need revelation from both. Being analytical by nature, it is easier for me to see the written Word, process it with my mind (soul), and know it came from God, than it is to hear something in my spirit, process it in my mind, and know the thought came from God.

I know I am not unique in this regard. After all, all of us have been trained from childhood to process information with our mind. We have attended years of school where we were

Yet, it is sad to say many of us have been in church our entire life and not been trained on how to process information provided to our spirit.

trained to take in information and use it to guide our decisions. That is a good thing. Yet sadly, many have been in church their entire lives and have still not been taught how to process information the Holy Spirit provides to their spirit to guide their decisions—a better thing. Scripture tells us we are a spirit; we live in a body; and we have a soul made up of our mind, our will, and our emotions. We have gyms where we can develop our bodies (a good thing); education and training to develop and manage our mind, will, and emotions (good things); but very little training in most churches on how to grow and develop our spirit. This must change if we are to walk in all that God has planned for us, both personally and professionally.

Step one to learning how to walk by the leading of the Holy Spirit is just as it is with the Word: you must first believe that God actually speaks to you through His Spirit talking to your spirit. You must take hearing from God by faith. It is not based on hearing a voice with your ears, a physical feeling, or deciphering the circumstances of the day. He speaks through the Holy Spirit to our spirit. Romans 8:16 (AMP) says: "The Spirit Himself [thus] testifies together with our own spirit, [assuring us] that we are children of God."

God's Holy Spirit speaks to our spirit. He does not speak to our mind. What He speaks must move from our spirit to our mind. We will talk about this more in a subsequent chapter, but let me share how it often happens for me. I will get a thought and then get an immediate "confirmation" from deep inside me. I will have a knowing or a peace about the thought. I just know the thought is true. The confirmation, or knowing, is coming from my spirit being prompted by the Holy Spirit. I may have been praying for weeks about a question or a situation, and suddenly I get a thought and an immediate confirmation from deep inside my spirit, and I will say to myself, "That's it. It is the answer to the prayer I've been bringing to God." I am sure many of you have had similar experiences. That is an example of the Holy Spirit speaking to your spirit and then your spirit initiating and confirming a thought based on the guidance you have received from the Holy Spirit.

Let's continue to look at the help the Holy Spirit provides to us. In 1 Corinthians 2:11–13 (AMP), Paul says:

> *For what person perceives (knows and understands) what passes through a man's thoughts except the man's own spirit within him? Just so no one discerns (comes to know and comprehend) the thoughts of God except the Spirit of God. Now we have not received the spirit [that belongs to] the world, but the [Holy] Spirit Who is from God, [given to us] that we might realize and comprehend and appreciate the gifts [of divine favor and blessing so freely and lavishly] bestowed on us by God. And we are setting these truths forth in words not taught by human wisdom but taught by the [Holy] Spirit, combining and interpreting spiritual truths*

with spiritual language [to those who possess the Holy Spirit].

This scripture tells us the Holy Spirit knows the thoughts of God. How often do we want to know the thoughts of God about a given situation? What confidence would *you* have in your decision if you *knew* God provided His thoughts on the decision? This scripture tells us the Holy Spirit knows what God's thoughts are and that God sent the Spirit to reveal them to us. That is awesome. What a promise. God will share His thoughts with us. Do you want a business advantage? What could possibly be more impactful than knowing God's thoughts about a situation? To receive it, we must learn how to sense God's direction, and we must take what we sense by faith.

Furthermore, the Word says God has given the Holy Spirit to us so we may know the gifts God has bestowed upon us. How often does the enemy try to convince you that God does not care about you? Or when God blesses someone, how often do you hear the enemy say, "Yeah, God did that for them, but they are holier than you are. You need to become a better person. You need to work harder to deserve it. Remember how you messed up yesterday? You can't ask for that now"? We need to remember that Jesus said He did not come to condemn us. If we are hearing thoughts of condemnation, they are coming from the enemy, and we should ignore them—always.

The Word says the Holy Spirit will help us recognize the enemy's words as lies. The Holy Spirit will provide promptings and leadings that, if followed, will make us "better people." What is a prompting or a leading? As I mentioned earlier, I will get a thought, and I will get a confirmation from deep inside that provides a knowing and a peace about it. I didn't get the knowing by getting the thought and reasoning it out in my mind or by doing a financial analysis to confirm its value. I get a confirmation/knowing in my spirit that the thought is from God. Or just the opposite may happen: I get a thought, and I get a "check" in my spirit that something is not right with that thought or direction for a given situation. I may not be able to articulate why I got the check and what the issue is, but I have learned to "stop" if I get the check.

Let's look at a couple of additional scriptures that provide more insight about the Holy Spirit:

> *A new heart will I give you and a new spirit will I put within you, and I will take away the stony heart out of your flesh and give you a heart of flesh. And I will put my Spirit within you and cause you to walk in My statutes, and you shall heed My ordinances and do them.*
>
> Ezekiel 36:26–27 (AMP)

> *What agreement [can there be between] a temple of God and idols? For we are the temple of the living God; even as God said, I will dwell in and with and among them and will walk in and with and among them, and I will be their God, and they shall be My people.*
>
> 2 Corinthians 6:16 (AMP)

These two scriptures talk about God's longing to have a relationship with His people. The passage in Ezekiel ties in very closely with what we learned from the parable of the sower in Mark 4. In Scripture, the terms *heart* and *spirit* are often used interchangeably. God says He will put a new spirit in us. That new spirit replaces the stony heart or stony ground that prevented the Word from producing a crop in our lives. Thank God that when we are born again, our spirit is reborn, and He gives us the ability to receive His Word so that it can grow in us.

God's Spirit in me, in combination with my reborn spirit, caused me to become excited about and understand what I read in His Word when I ask Him to show me if His Word is real. In 2 Corinthians, Paul tells us that God will dwell in us and guide us. How does He do that? These scriptures tell us that God, by His Holy Spirit, has made our hearts new and has made them good ground to sow the Word of God into us. That good ground results in a thirty-, a sixty-, and a one-hundred-fold return on the seed of the Word sown as we stand in faith and act on it.

You may say, "That is all well and good, but I don't think I have the Holy Spirit in me," or you may ask, "How can I know if I do?" If you are a follower of Christ, Acts 2:38–39 provides the answer:

> *Then Peter said unto them, Repent, and be baptized every one of you in the name of Jesus Christ for the remission of sins, and ye shall receive the gift of the Holy Ghost. For the promise is unto you, and to your children, and to all that are afar off, even as many as the Lord our God shall call.*

If you have received Jesus as your Savior and repented of your sins, you have received the Holy Spirit. It is a gift that Jesus' sacrifice provides to anyone who will receive Him. As the

No matter what you do, God's Holy Spirit will not leave you.

passage from 2 Corinthians says, God has given us His Spirit to live in and direct us. It is also why Jesus can say, "I will never leave you or forsake you." Once we accept Jesus as our Lord and Savior, God's Spirit takes up residence in us, and He will never leave us. What an amazing thing. Don't let religious ideas steal this truth from you. *No matter what you do, God's Holy Spirit will not leave you.* He is not there just when you are doing the "right things" or religious activities. It is not based on anything you do right or wrong. It is a gift and one that will never be taken back, but we must receive it by faith. We must believe it is true.

It is up to us to develop a relationship with the Holy Spirit so we can recognize His leading and know God's will in every situation, so we can know and aspire to bring the wisdom of God to every situation we face, and so we can know how to release His power to bless those around us. I've been learning how to better sense and respond to the leading of the Holy Spirit for almost thirty years. I still don't hear God speaking to me in every situation. Sometimes I get busy and don't think to ask. Other times it is because I don't spend time listening to God. I get caught up in the busyness of life—the cares of this world. But God is loving and merciful, He always responds when I make time for Him, and He will do the same for you. The Bible says He is no respecter of persons.

Developing our ability to sense His direction is a process, just like the process we use to develop our mind. We don't take college courses when we are five years old. We learn very basic things, apply them, and then add more knowledge and experience each year. By the way, there is also an element of faith involved in the education process. It is faith in the process and the potential benefits that come with years of study that cause people to invest tens, if not hundreds of thousands of dollars and thousands of hours into education, believing it will eventually benefit them economically. Again, there is nothing wrong with that if it aligns with God's will for your life. However, what I am talking about will provide a much bigger "payoff" to those who invest the time to develop a relationship with the Holy Spirit. We need to accept by faith that the investment of our time studying and growing in the knowledge of spiritual principles will produce outcomes for our good and the good of others.

We must realize that God provides confirmation of revelations in His Word via the Holy Spirit in us and that His Spirit talks and ministers with our spirit to provide His truth and wisdom about all things. I'm sure nearly all of us who are searching the things of God have experienced something similar to this. You are reading the Bible, land on a scripture, something inside you "clicks," and you say to yourself, "Wow! This is the truth," or "This is the answer I've been praying for," or "This is right." You didn't get that confirmation from your mind. You "sensed" it come from deep inside you, and you just knew it was right. That is an example of the Holy Spirit confirming God's Word to our spirit.

Let's look at the ways in which the Holy Spirit ministers to us. In John 14:16–17 (AMP), Jesus says:

> *And I will ask the Father, and He will give you another Comforter (Counselor, Helper, Intercessor, Advocate, Strengthener, and Standby), that He may remain with you forever—The Spirit of Truth, Whom the world cannot receive (welcome, take to its heart), because it does not see Him or know and recognize Him. But you know and recognize Him, for He lives with you [constantly] and will be in you.*

Jesus is telling His disciples and us that He is going to ask the Father, and the Father will give us another Comforter (the Holy Spirit), who will remain with us forever. Do you think that God answers Jesus' requests? Is there a single account in Scripture where He doesn't? Of course not; how could there be? Jesus said He only says what the Father tells Him to say and only does what the Father tells Him to do. If you have accepted Jesus as your Lord and Savior, then the Holy Spirit lives in you. You are not a special exception. You may not be aware of it, but it is still true, nonetheless. The scripture goes on to say He lives with you constantly.

In John 14:26 (AMP), Jesus provides more insight into the counsel the Holy Spirit provides:

> *But the Comforter (Counselor, Helper, Intercessor, Advocate, Strengthener, Standby), the Holy Spirit, Whom the Father will send in My name [in My place, to represent Me and act on My behalf], He will teach you all things. And He will cause you to recall (will remind you of, bring to your remembrance) everything I have told you.*

The Father sends the Holy Spirit to teach us all things. "All things" leaves nothing out. Do you want to know how to do your job better or be a more effective leader? Do you want to know how to be a better spouse? The Holy Spirit will teach you. Spend time with Him in prayer, and He will provide wisdom to make you more effective in everything you do. Remember, it is based on the measure you mete. Will you seek God's guidance in all areas of your life?

Jesus does not exaggerate; He used the word *all*. We need to decide if we are going to take Jesus at His Word. Like everything that is in the Word of God, we must take it by faith. Once we do, we should expect the Holy Spirit to counsel us in all areas. As previously stated, if you are a born-again believer in Jesus, the Holy Spirit is already in you. If you are not, change that right now by asking Jesus to forgive you of your sins and tell Him you want to have a relationship with Him. That's all it takes; it happens that fast. If you humbled yourself, admitted you've sinned, and prayed that prayer, God's Holy Spirit is in you right now.

The Word says the Holy Spirit is always speaking to us. He may not be speaking to you on a topic at the top of your prayer list, and you may think, "God is not talking to me." However, just because it is the most important topic to you, that doesn't mean it's the most important topic to God for you. He is going to talk to us about the most impactful topic, whether we realize it or not. We need to learn how to listen. We are not going to hear Him with our natural ears. We are going to hear (sense) Him with our spirit. In John 16:7 (AMP), Jesus tells us plainly that once He leaves, is crucified, and raised from the dead, He will send us the Holy Spirit.

> *However, I am telling you nothing but the truth when I say it is profitable (good, expedient, advantageous) for you that I go away. Because if I do not go away, the Comforter (Counselor, Helper, Advocate, Intercessor, Strengthener, Standby) will not come to you [into close fellowship with you]; but if I go away, I will send Him to you [to be in close fellowship with you].*

The Holy Spirit who lives in us provides us the thoughts of the one who knows all, who guides us into all truth! How amazing is that. All we need for success in life has been given to us through the price Jesus paid on the cross. If we can hear the guidance the Holy Spirit provides about each situation we face and

If we can hear what the Holy Spirit thinks about a situation, we will never make a wrong decision.

then obey it, we will never make a wrong decision. That is worth repeating. If we can hear the guidance the Holy Spirit provides about each situation we face and then obey it, we will never make a wrong decision. If you want an advantage in the business world, consistently seek and follow the leading of the Holy Spirit.

You can have twenty people with fifteen degrees each working for you, but there is one thing all their education combined will not be able to do—predict the future. God doesn't predict the future; He *knows* the future, and His answers and instruction always take that into account. God has a plan for us, and He always provides guidance with our futures in mind. That does not mean He is going to show us the future (He may), but He will always provide answers and guidance that position us appropriately for the future. We need to be tuned in to listen. I have found that God's leading happens little by little, step by step. For example, He may lead you into a job that does not seem all that significant today, but you take it because you believe He is leading you in that direction. Two years later, you have some highly marketable skills you can use in a hot segment of a market.

When God says He will show you the future, that doesn't always mean you will actually "see into the future." Once you arrive in the future, though, you will see how well the decisions you made positioned you for your new environment. Many times in my career, I have made decisions, defined solutions, and defined processes only to find out two years later how perfectly they aligned with where the marketplace had evolved. In some cases, I had no idea when I made those decisions how well they would position me, my organization, or my clients for the future, but God did. I found myself in such a good spot because the decisions I had made two years earlier were aligned with where God was leading me via the Holy Spirit.

In nearly every case, God didn't show me the end result, and I'm glad he didn't. If He had, I would have screwed it up trying to use my limited understanding and resources to make something happen quicker. But He did provide me step-by-step guidance that didn't always seem all that relevant, but now I'm in the middle of the hottest segment of the market I serve. As I mentioned, I started my career as an engineer working on the Space Shuttle program. My plan was to get a master's degree in electrical engineering and grow my engineering expertise. I even started taking master's classes to increase my expertise. God changed my path and led me step by step over many years until I found myself the senior leader of an analytics and information management consulting practice.

Analytics and information management encapsulates many of the big buzzwords in the industry today, such as cognitive computing, big data, artificial intelligence, machine learning, and advanced analytics. I would have never had the insight or foresight to direct myself to that discipline. As a matter of fact, I didn't even know what a consultant was until I was in my mid-thirties. Yet, I found myself leading a consulting practice in one of the hottest segments of the market. God, by His Holy Spirit, led me to that spot. I am certain there were many times along the way I didn't hear what He was telling me. Or worse, I heard Him and didn't do what He told me. Yet, the good news is God loves us and is full of grace. He never gives up on us, and I never gave up on Him. Consequently, I found myself in a place I never would have envisioned on my own. God is awesome, and God is no respecter of persons. What He has done for me, He can and will do for you if you believe He can and will.

As a born-again believer, you have the one who knows the future in you, and He is willing to tell you about that future now. It is so important for us to meditate on these scriptures, ask God for His help in understanding how to sense the leading of the Holy Spirit, and believe He is leading us. Jesus said, "my sheep hear my voice." He *will* teach you and show you. It is His desire to fellowship with His children. Jesus paid the ultimate price so we could have that fellowship. We need to remember that when the enemy is telling us "God doesn't care," "He won't talk with you," "You're too insignificant," "He doesn't have time for you," or "You can't hear from God," it is a lie, so don't believe it. Jesus suffered so that anyone who would believe could have a relationship with the Father through the Holy Spirit.

We are not always going to get the hearing part right. Over time, we learn how to be better at hearing from the Holy Spirit. God knows our hearts, and He will help clean up any mess we create as we're trying to hear from Him and stepping out to do something when, in fact, we didn't clearly hear from Him.

After I had been working at the Space Center for five years, I started to get the sense it was time to move on. Consequently, I started to look for my next job. After a short time and a lot of prayer, I concluded that Washington, DC, might be the place I should focus my search. So, I would go to the library every week and get a copy of the Sunday *Washington Post* (this was many years ago, before the Internet), and I would send out résumés each week in response to the employment ads.

After a few months, I received a couple of potential opportunities, so I coordinated a trip to DC to interview with those firms. The interviews went well, and I was very excited to be moving on to the next stage of my career, believing I was taking the next step God had for me. My thoughts were, *God is moving me to the next level; this is great.* Moving to DC was very exciting to me, but not so much so for my wife. We had a three-year-old son and a one-year-old daughter, and we would be moving away from her family to an area where we had no support system. I knew that was scary for her, but I also knew it was a new challenge in an exciting new area, so if it was God's will, I knew it would be best for us.

I returned home, all excited after the interviews, and I'm sure my excitement just made her more nervous. Within a couple of days, I got a job offer from one of the companies. I was so thrilled. I told them I would take a couple of days to consider it and get back to them. I shared the news with my wife. She wasn't as excited as I was, but she was willing to go if I thought we should. I wasn't 100 percent sure it was God's will for me to take that particular job, but I wanted to be. So later that night, I was lying on the floor, praying (nothing spiritual about lying on the floor; it was late, and I was tired), and I said to God, "You know I am ready and want to move on to something else. I want to do this, but I really don't know if this is Your will. Above all, I want to do Your will. I have an open door, and I don't know what else to do but walk through the door. If it is not Your will, have them rescind the offer." A simple prayer, and I truly meant it, and God knew I meant it.

The next day, I got a call from the firm, and they rescinded the offer. The recruiter actually used the word rescind in our discussion. That was the only time in my career a job offer had ever been pulled back. This is a great example of being careful of what you pray for—just kidding. On the one hand, I was so disappointed because I was ready to move on. But on the other hand, I knew God was involved, and I knew what His will was. I was so thankful that He heard and answered my prayer.

I tell you that story for two reasons. First, God wants us to know His will and hear from the Holy Spirit in these situations, so we know what to do. At the time, I did not know how to hear from God like I do today, and I expect to be able to hear better next year and the year after that. I heard the move to Washington, DC, part correctly, though, because a year later, I got another offer, the *right* offer, and we moved to DC. So, I'd heard the DC part right, but in my excitement, I didn't ask about the timing and the right job until after I received the offer. I thank God for His mercy. He stepped in because I asked, and He prevented me from making a big mistake. I truly believe that if I hadn't asked, He would have allowed me to take the first offer.

God is very specific in His guidance. It wasn't just about moving to DC; it was about what job to take and when to move to DC. The original offer was an engineering role. The role the following year provided my introduction to consulting. It changed my career trajectory, and I'm pretty sure I would not be where I am today had I taken the original offer.

Second, God is a loving God, full of grace, and He knows our hearts. We won't always clearly hear what He is saying, but if our hearts are right, His grace will cover us. Mine was a simple, unsophisticated prayer, and His answer kept me from making a big mistake and getting out of His will.

We cannot let the fear of "missing it" cause us to turn our backs on hearing from the Holy Spirit and acting on what we hear in faith. That is what the enemy wants. He will do all he can to convince you that you can't hear from God or that what you heard is not really from God. Believers walking in the guidance and power of the Holy Spirit is what the enemy fears the most. Only by bringing our whole self (body, soul, and *spirit*) to the workplace will we maximize our impact on our clients, customers, colleagues, and businesses. The enemy knows there is a level of impact we can have that he can't stop when the Holy Spirit is leading us. It is an impact that clearly differentiates us from others, not because we are smarter or more talented, but because we have access to an information source far more comprehensive than Google and YouTube combined.

The Holy Spirit also ministers to us as a helper in prayer. In Romans 8:26–27 (KJV), Paul tells us how the Holy Spirit intercedes for us in prayer:

> *Likewise the Spirit also helpeth our infirmities: for we know not what we should pray for as we ought: but the Spirit itself maketh intercession for us with groanings which cannot be uttered. And he that searcheth the hearts knoweth what is the mind of the Spirit, because he maketh intercession for the saints according to the will of God.*

This is one of the most powerful passages I have stood upon in my life. I confess and trust that the Holy Spirit will intercede and pray God's perfect will for me. My goodness, what a promise that is. God will pray His perfect will for us through the Holy Spirit. God praying for me! Meditate on that for a while.

I know if I pray just with my mind, I can sometimes hear fear or worry creep into my prayers. I also know that at times I can't be sure the motives behind my prayers are always as pure as I would like to think. Most importantly, I can pray only for those things that I am aware of. I don't know what is happening in my children's lives when I am not around. I don't know what is happening with my wife. I don't know what is happening with my clients or team members. I can pray only about things that my mind (soul) is aware of. Even when I have specific things to take to the Lord in prayer, once I have prayed the Word over a situation, I'm done. I don't know what else to pray. I will continue to confess God's Word in prayer each day, but that only takes a few minutes.

Another thing to consider is I can't trust my soul to pray for all that I require. It is impossible for me to know everything I need to pray for simply because I don't know the future. I can sow the Word, but I don't know every situation that is coming that I need to pray about. God does, and He will use the Holy Spirit to pray His perfect will for me and others through me if I let Him. I must set aside time just to let the Holy Spirit pray through me. I'm not suggesting that if we are perfect at allowing the Holy Spirit to pray for us that we will never have any problems. That is not scriptural. Jesus told us we will have tribulations in this world. But I am convinced that praying in the Spirit will help us avoid many of those tribulations and successfully walk through them in faith and love when they occur.

Furthermore, it allows God to pray His perfect will for others through us. Again, it is not just about me. God knows where people in my life are struggling, even when I don't. He can use me to pray for their situations, and most importantly, He can show me what to do to demonstrate His love toward them. How do I pray in the Spirit? First Corinthians 14:14 (AMP) tells us: "For if I pray in an [unknown] tongue, my spirit [by the Holy Spirit within me] prays, but my mind is unproductive [it bears no fruit and helps nobody]."

When I pray in tongues, my mind does not know what I am praying about, but my spirit, led by the Holy Spirit, does. I know that makes many uncomfortable, but it is scriptural, it is powerful, and it is available to anyone who will believe. I must say this again: the scripture says that God via the Holy Spirit will pray His will for you. God will pray for you! Amazing, who would not want that in their lives? Don't let the enemy steal that from you.

I spent many years on the road and away from my family for four or five days a week. I would set aside time most mornings to pray for my family. Often I didn't know exactly what to pray to help them that day. I wasn't at home, so I didn't know the challenge each person in my home was facing, but the Holy Spirit did, and when I allowed Him to pray through me, I was praying for things that were going on with each of them. I would like to say I was extremely diligent and that I prayed for them in the Spirit every day, but I didn't. At times, I let the cares of the day creep in. However, I know God honored me when I did. I have learned how important this is to my life and the lives of those I am surrounded by; therefore, it is an area I continue to work at and grow in.

As I said, and scripture confirms, if I am praying in the Spirit, I may not even know what I am praying about, but that is okay. That is actually the point: I don't know everything, and even if I was aware, I could misread a situation and pray incorrectly. This is part of what God means when He tells us to be humble. Part of being humble is recognizing you don't know everything, and even those things you are highly educated in, you don't know as much as the Creator of the universe. Because we know that God knows best, we come before Him, knowing that He knows what and who we should be praying for. Those prayers kept my children from many of the traps the enemy had set for them and kept my family together during the years I was on the road.

On many occasions, I have prayed in the Spirit before going into a big meeting. I pray and confess His Word to expect His favor to be upon me and to provide me with insight about how to manage a room. Then I pray for His wisdom to be available to me, and then I will pray in the Spirit for the meeting. I do this by faith to allow God to pray His perfect will over the situation I am faced with. Some of the interactions in a meeting can be very emotionally intense. However, I am able to appear calm when others are clearly stressed. Over and over again, God has provided an answer to the situation in "real time." Even though my mind may have been trying to get my emotions to run as hot as everyone else's, but I wasn't looking for the answer just with my mind. I was listening for my spirit to hear the Holy Spirit provide and confirm the answer, and He has on many occasions. The key was not listing to all the fear and strife but listening and trusting that the Holy Spirit was going to provide the answer. We must believe that and then practice hearing so that when we get in those intense situations, we know how to hear God's guidance through the still, small voice of our spirit amidst all the clamor going on in the room and in our mind.

I may never know all the times I missed what God was saying; however, I know there were many times where God provided and confirmed a thought that changed the dynamics in the room or solved a challenge the group in the room was faced with. Interestingly, when God provides His wisdom in those situations, others often interpret it as intelligence or knowledge. On more than one occasion, individuals have asked me, "How did you figure that out?" When you step back and think about it, why wouldn't someone see it as knowledge? He knows everything about everything, and as we have learned, He wants to share that with His people (you and me). How great is that? What an advantage we have through our relationship with the Holy Spirit, and that is why it is so important that we bring our spiritual self to our vocation. In a later chapter, we will discuss more about how to develop and mature that relationship and our ability to recognize His guidance.

The third area the Holy Spirit provides us with help is in accessing God's power. Below are scriptures that confirm God's desire for us to walk in His power and the role the Holy Spirit plays in allowing us to do so:

> *The earth was without form and an empty waste, and darkness was upon the face of the very great deep. The Spirit of God was moving (hovering, brooding) over the face of the waters. And God said, Let there be light; and there was light.*

> Genesis 1:2–3 (AMP)

> *"But you shall receive power (ability, efficiency, and might) when the Holy Spirit has come upon you, and you shall be My witnesses in Jerusalem and all Judea and Samaria and to the ends (the very bounds) of the earth."*

> Acts 1:8 (AMP)

And it shall come to pass in the last days, God declares,
that I will pour out of My Spirit upon all mankind,
and your sons and your daughters shall prophesy
[telling forth the divine counsels] and your young men
shall see visions (divinely granted appearances), and
your old men shall dream [divinely suggested] dreams.

Acts 2:17 (AMP)

"This is because I have never spoken on My own
authority or of My own accord or as self-appointed, but
the Father Who sent Me has Himself given Me orders
[concerning] what to say and what to tell."

John 12:49 (AMP)

How do you activate the power of the Holy Spirit? Power to do what? The scripture says the power to be His witnesses to the ends of the earth. Certainly, that includes actually witnessing to individuals in one-on-one conversations. But as we have discussed, it is also the power to be a witness, to walk in, and to stand on the Word, no matter how difficult the immediate circumstances are, and bring God's blessing to pass in that situation.

We see the process defined in Genesis 1:2–3. God speaks, and the Holy Spirit responds to His words in power to produce change in the physical realm. This truth holds for us, as well. By faith, we speak God's Word over a situation, and the Holy Spirit in us responds to God's Word to produce change in the physical realm around us. Now can you see why the enemy is so diligent about stealing the Word from us? Once we speak God's Word consistently over a situation in faith, the Holy Spirit responds to God's Word, and there is nothing the enemy can do to stop it from coming to pass.

The Holy Spirit will always respond to the Word of God. We can stop it only if we allow the pressures of the day to get our focus off the Word and change our confession to focus on the circumstances or problem and not God's promises. The Bible tells us, having done all to stand, we must stand. We stand in faith in the promises of God. We stand until the expected result manifests. This could require us to stand for years. As I mentioned in the account above, I waited nearly two years until the right opportunity in the right place came along. It was not easy. I wanted to move on badly. I sowed the Word, and the Holy Spirit led me in His timing to the right outcome. I did not give up when the first opportunity didn't work out.

Your sons and daughters shall prophesy, and old men shall dream dreams. We saw Daniel and Joseph getting revelation by the Spirit to interpret situations their leaders faced, and they were the only ones who had the answers. It resulted in prosperity for them and for entire nations. On multiple occasions, God has provided me His wisdom in situations where folks were confused and looking for answers. He did not do that because of my holiness. He wanted to provide it out of His love for those individuals and me. He provided it to me simply because I asked Him and then spent time listening. I'll say it again: He will do it for any born-again believer. The Bible says He is no respecter of persons.

I was helping a Fortune Five company rationalize how data was being managed and used post-merger. It was an enormous challenge that required some real insight into how to attack something very large and complex. I mean, where do you start when you are merging three large companies at once? My team was asked to do a strategy project to help the client come up with an approach to integrate and manage the data to support the operations of a single company. So, we used a typical consulting gig approach, performed a current state assessment, defined a target state, and then created a roadmap that described how to take the organization from the current state to the target state.

But we also needed to determine if there was a business case to support a broader rationalization of the data management operations across the three distinct organizations and if there was, how would we sequence such an effort? We were weeks into the project, and I was interviewing the person who reported the merger progress to Wall Street to understand the process used to generate the financial reports that measured merger progress. A few days after the discussion, I heard two words come to me: "market cap." I don't mean I heard an audible voice, but the phrase came to my mind, and I received that knowing from the inside that I previously mentioned.

I reached out to analysts in my firm and requested they perform an analysis of what happens to an organization's market capitalization over a two-year period if earnings are misreported to Wall Street. They came back to me and told me that, on average, companies could expect to see an 18 percent dip in their market capitalization. At the time, this was a $200-plus billion-dollar company, which would mean close to a $40 billion hit to their market capitalization if they misreported the data—confirmation that it was important.

Fast forward a couple of weeks, we had to report to the senior vice president in charge of finance for the organization. When we got to that slide in the presentation, and as I started to discuss, the client said, "I am so worried about this, and nobody else is talking to me about it." I knew at that point we had found what they considered the key concern, and we would get the opportunity to help them work through it. I was so happy we were going to close a new deal. A leader in my organization asked, "How did you think of that?"

I think I said, "It just kind of came to me." I knew where it came from, and as I said earlier, when you receive insight from the Holy Spirit, others will attribute that to intelligence and think you are smart.

That is not the end of the story, however. As I mentioned, I was so happy the insight had turned into a new opportunity for us as a firm and that I was getting the credit for it. I was so thankful to God for providing me that insight, for the opportunity, and for that business success. However, I'm embarrassed to say how long it took me to understand what was really going on in that situation. God finally came out and plainly told me a few years later. He said, "I did not give you that insight to bless you so you could sell more business. I gave you that insight to bless your client."

Remember the quote, "I am so worried about this, and no one is talking to me about it"?

God told me from my spirit, "I sent you there to talk to them about it." I would have never considered discussing that topic if it had not come from God.

I didn't see His purpose clearly because I was more focused on my personal success. It was a tremendous lesson for me to know that God gives revelation specific to a need. However, He gives it not so I can be blessed, but so I can help others with things that no one else may be aware of. In that process, my firm and I will be blessed by additional business, but the main focus is not about me and my success. It is about meeting the needs of others— my client in this case. It is about bringing God's wisdom and knowledge to minister and serve them. I need to keep reminding myself it's not about me. I can say from experience that as you continue to obtain more and more influence, it becomes more and more difficult to keep the focus off you because so many are putting it on you.

I have many more examples of the Holy Spirit providing me the wisdom to know what to focus on in a very complex environment. Walking with the Holy Spirit is not a black-and-white thing. We can read the Word and most of the time be reasonably certain about what it is telling us. Hearing from the Holy Spirit is a completely different thing.

It is not easy to always know what the Holy Spirit is saying (many times we will ask ourselves, "Was that the Holy Spirit, or was it just me?"), and we will mess up sometimes and move out on something that was just us and not inspired by the Spirit. Or, out of fear or confusion, we may not act on something the Holy Spirit provided, and that could produce some challenging circumstances. However, that doesn't mean we should stop learning and moving forward. When you were training your mind in school, you didn't quit because you got a wrong answer on a test. You used the test to determine how well you understood the subject and moved on by addressing the gaps in your understanding highlighted via the test you took.

Similarly, as you begin to seek guidance from the Holy Spirit, start with the small things to gain experience. Nothing is too small for God. If it matters to you, it matters to Him, and He will provide guidance. Practice asking for God's wisdom daily and listening to your spirit for answers to the questions and challenges of the day. As it is with anything, the more we do it, the more experienced we get at it, and the easier it becomes to recognize His voice. We cannot let the fear of messing up get in the way of the power and impact that comes from being led by the Holy Spirit. God wants to use you to impact the lives of many, and He releases His power to do it through His Holy Spirit.

The world needs to see it and needs to be blessed by it. In Section Three of this book, we are going to talk more about how to operate daily in the power and guidance of the Holy Spirit as we navigate our professional lives.

CHAPTER 5

Grace—God's Unmerited Favor

*[All] are justified and made upright and in right
standing with God, freely and gratuitously by His grace
(His unmerited favor and mercy), through the redemption which is [provided] in Christ Jesus.*

Romans 3:24 (AMP)

It has taken me more than twenty-five years to get an understanding of how fundamental grace is to the freedom a relationship
with Jesus provides. That's not to suggest I completely understand what it means today. However, I have learned enough over
the past few years to obtain a level of freedom I had not previously experienced, specifically, freedom from guilt, self-condemnation, and thoughts of inadequacy.

I remember studying the Word in the early nineties, and the
Holy Spirit showing me that grace was more than a salutation
used in the introduction of Paul's letters to the churches. He
began to show me that it was a spiritual force. When I read Paul's
account of the thorn in the flesh, I could see that God was telling
Paul to use grace. From that, I could see that grace was tangible
and had an element of power to it. After all, God was telling Paul
to put it to use. But I didn't really understand how to apply it in
my life and what to expect if I did. In his account, Paul asked
God to remove the thorn, and God responded by saying that His

grace is sufficient (2 Corinthians 12:7). I later came to understand that faith in God's grace is a spiritual force available to us to thwart the attacks and lies of the enemy, and it is fundamental to my ability to believe God's promises are for me and to see those promises come to fruition.

So why are we talking about it with respect to our calling in the business realm? Because it is directly tied to our righteousness (right standing with God), and we are going to see what the righteous have access to in our relationship with God. For now, consider this: if I am walking around feeling guilty and unworthy all the time, how does that affect my confidence in decision-making? What does it do to my ability to lead others effectively? If I feel I am constantly missing the mark due to my inability to keep all the rules that religion tells me I must observe to remain in right standing with God, how does that affect my relationship with God and my relationship with others? Can I really have the faith to believe that God has my back if I don't think God is happy with me? Do I restrict what God and the Holy Spirit want to do through me in my professional role to bless others because I do not feel righteous enough to earn His help?

For years this type of thinking impacted what I would ask God for and when I would ask it. My thinking was, *I've sinned; I can't ask God for help now.* Or, *I did three good things today; now I can ask God for help.* Have you had similar thoughts? I would be surprised if you didn't. It is a common ploy of the enemy. For me, so much of that thinking was based on my religious upbringing. I was keeping score. *If I do enough good and the scoreboard looks positive, then God will be pleased with me, and I can go to Him and ask for help.* The challenge is determining how much is "good enough."

The enemy will tell you that you've never done enough. He will always point out where you come up short. He is in the condemnation business. The Bible tells us we can never be in right standing with God based on our good works because we will *always* come up short. While God is pleased with the good works we do (if our motives are right—more on that later), our good works will not make us righteous in God's eyes. However, those good acts can make us pleasing in His eyes. Those are two very different things, and it is important not to confuse them.

Religion tells us that works (keeping the Jewish law or all the rules created by any religious sect or Christian denomination) will provide us right standing with God. But that is the very thing that Jesus challenged the religious leaders on in His day. He lifted Himself up and said unto them, "He that is without sin among you, let him first cast a stone at her." Even though many in the crowd were ardent students of the Law and religious leaders, they all knew they had sinned and dropped their stones and walked away. Grace tells us we can't keep all the Law. The good news is the redemption we need (being saved from sin) has been provided through the gift of grace received through our faith in Jesus Christ. Religion will work you to death, trying to obtain right standing with God. Grace, on the other hand, provides peace and rest because you understand that you've obtained right standing with God

Religion will work you to death, trying to obtain right standing with God. Grace, in contrast, provides peace and rest because you understand that you've obtained right standing with God through the sacrifice of Jesus on the cross.

through the sacrifice of Jesus on the cross, which is not based on any good thing you've done.

A religious mindset says, "I need to do more so that God is pleased with me," and a grace mindset says, "There is not one thing I can do to make God love me more than He already does." What is grace? As one would expect, the Scripture provides us the definition:

> *For while the Law was given through Moses, grace*
> *(unearned, undeserved favor and spiritual blessing)*
> *and truth came through Jesus Christ.*

> John 1:17 (AMP)

> *[All] are justified and made upright and in right*
> *standing with God, freely and gratuitously by His grace*
> *(His unmerited favor and mercy), through the redemp-*
> *tion which is [provided] in Christ Jesus.*

> Romans 3:24 (AMP)

Grace, God's unmerited favor and mercy, is a gift we do not deserve. Yet it is one that is freely given, and we must receive. The redemptive act of Jesus Christ's sacrifice on the cross released God's unmerited favor and mercy to us.

It is God's grace through faith in Jesus and His sacrifice that made us and keeps us in right standing with God. I am choosing my words carefully here; it makes us and keeps us in right standing with God. Right standing with God is not living in guilt and condemnation. I am convinced via my study of the Bible that it is God's desire for us to *never* live another minute in guilt and condemnation for the rest of our lives. How freeing is that? I realize that is a big statement, and it could make religious people's heads explode, but it is scriptural. What measure will you mete? While I can't say I never walk around in guilt and condemnation, I can say I do it a lot less now than I did in the past, and it is wonderful! The good news is (and the gospel is the good news) that grace is available to all who believe Jesus died, rose again, and in doing so, provided His right standing with God to us.

God is no respecter of persons; He makes His right standing available to all. How much better news could you get? How do we receive grace? Ephesians 2:8 (AMP) tells us: "For it is by free grace (God's unmerited favor) that you are saved (delivered from judgment *and* made partakers of Christ's salvation) through [your] faith. And this [salvation] is not of yourselves [of your own doing, it came not through your own striving], but it is the gift of God."

How do you receive it? Just like everything else with God, you receive it by faith. This was a tough one to fully get my head around and to get into my spirit because my religious teaching got in the way. I was free from God's judgment, but I was not free from *my* judgment and condemnation. It is impossible to believe all of God's promises when you are walking around in self-condemnation. I found myself rationalizing that I was good enough to believe some of God's promises but not good enough to believe everything. I thought I needed to clean up my sin and do better before I could believe the "really big" promises. The Bible tells us we are to judge ourselves, but it does not say we are to condemn ourselves. If we sin, we are to admit it (judge it), confess it, repent of it, and believe the Word, which says God is faithful to forgive us our sin, and He remembers it no more.

From that point, we move on in right standing with God. What good news!

I struggled to believe there was nothing I could do other than repent and ask forgiveness. Surely God must require me to make some kind of sacrifice to get in line with His plan. That thinking was partially correct. It does require a sacrifice; however, Jesus is the one who provided that sacrifice. My part in the equation is to put aside my pride (humble myself), admit my mistakes, repent, believe forgiveness is available, and accept it. One of the biggest hurdles to overcome while trying to walk in grace is our pride, our belief that if we work hard enough, we can be good enough to earn God's blessings. The Word tells us we can't, our experience shows us we can't, and yet pride tells us we can. As long as we think we can, we will be caught in the miserable cycle of our pride pushing us to work harder at doing good things we will inevitably mess up. The enemy will jump in and pour the condemnation on us, we will suffer under it for a while, and then we will finally make the decision to try even harder the next time. Does this pattern sound familiar? Is there any freedom in that? I am exhausted just thinking about it. Letting go of believing that doing good works earns us right standing with God and placing our faith in God's grace breaks that wicked cycle.

I remember in the early '90s when I asked God about the power of grace. He started by showing me that I was free from condemnation. The Word says Jesus did not come to condemn; Satan is the condemner. Surprisingly, one of the most difficult aspects of not walking around in condemnation was the reactions to this truth that I perceived from other Christians (I'm sure my perception was not always true). You may find as you walk around not condemning yourself every time you make a mistake that some of your Christian friends may start wondering who you think you are. They may say, "I saw what you did yesterday. How can you act like you deserve anything from God?" I had to decide whether I believed what the Word says or whether I was going to let people's opinions shape what I believed. I decided to follow the Word. It took some time to get to the point where I believed God was not condemning me for my actions. However, I was still working hard to do what was "right." It took me a lot longer to understand that grace is a gift, and it is not earned.

If you've been attending church for many years, you've probably heard countless times that we can't be good enough to earn right standing with God. That can be a very depressing sermon if it is not followed by a discussion of grace. Walking away knowing we can't do enough to earn right standing with God will make us feel defeated unless we are also taught that God's grace has put us in right standing, and our part is to receive it by faith. Our rest comes in knowing that Jesus paid for all of our sins: the sins we committed before we were saved, the ones we have committed since we have been saved, and the ones we will commit in the future. All we have to do is repent and ask forgiveness. That type of thinking is really hard for many of us because our culture teaches us (especially in the business world) that we must earn our place, we must earn someone's respect, and we must earn someone's love.

Yet grace is a gift we must receive; it is impossible to earn. All those years, I had in my mind a picture of a big scoreboard. On one side was the number of my good deeds; on the other side was the number of my sins. Before I was saved, the number on the sin side was a lot bigger than the number of good deeds. So, I was losing the game. When I accepted Christ, I knew that He had forgiven all my sins, and the score on the sin side went to zero. Because I didn't have a real understanding of God's grace, I started my work to sin less and do more good things so that the scoreboard on the good works' side showed that I was a good person and a follower of God. This type of thinking is well-intentioned but leads to many bad behaviors.

For one, I thought I could just sit back and take pride in the fact that my scoreboard was showing me to be a winner. Even worse, at times, I would compare my scoreboard with what I perceived other people's scoreboards showed. I felt good (prideful) when I perceived my score was higher than others and felt condemned when I thought my score was lower than others.

Out of pride, that would cause me to go back to work to try and ring up some additional good points on the scoreboard to feel better about myself. But that only exhausted me, frustrated me, and made me very hard to get along with. There was no freedom in that. I had been deceived into thinking my efforts could produce righteousness.

Sinning less and doing good works are the right goals. I just had the wrong motivation for doing both. It was about making myself better, not loving and trusting God. The focus was still on me and my performance, not on the gift God had given me and how my good works could be a method of sharing God's love with others. After all, how could I share God's love with others if I didn't think He loved me, or I had to do twenty things before He would love me again after I messed up?

The scripture says once we accept Jesus as Lord and Savior, our sins *are* forgiven, not *were* forgiven. That means all sins past, present, and future. What I finally realized after many years of working to prove myself worthy is that when I got saved, God blew up the scoreboard. Nobody but the devil is keeping score. I already won. In God's eyes, I am already what and who He says I am, independent of my performance. God sees me as He intends me to be; He sees me through faith. Every time I mess up, the devil comes to tell me things like, "You don't deserve what you are believing. You've got to do X to earn God's promises now."

The truth is once I ask God for forgiveness for my sins, according to the Word, He no longer remembers them. But the accuser does, and he will pester us with lies over and over again until we shut him down. How do we do that? Speak God's promises to him, using the sword of the Spirit—the Word of God. Tell him, according to the Word, "My righteousness is based on what Jesus has done, not what I have done." Resist him, and he will flee.

When people sinned under the old covenant, the sin caused them to be separated from God. That was what the Law taught. However, in the New Testament, Jesus said, "I will never leave you or forsake you." We know He sent His Holy Spirit to live in us once we were born again, and from Scripture, we know the Holy Spirit never leaves. That can only be possible because God's grace covers not only our past sins but our future sins, as well. If it didn't, the Holy Spirit would not be able to reside within us. If we are seeking God, there is no sin we can commit that will cause God to break our constant fellowship and right standing with Him. If the fellowship is broken, it is because we are not walking in it. We've pulled back, or worse yet, rejected it. It is a tactic of the devil to convince us we are unworthy and can't talk to God. It is a lie!

I pulled back from God and His promises due to guilt and condemnation. The enemy uses guilt and condemnation to make us ashamed, just as he did to Adam and Eve in the garden. After they sinned, the Bible says they were afraid and hid from God. The enemy has no new tactics. He will try to get us to hide from God too. It is up to us to build our faith in this area and believe that when we mess up, we can immediately humble ourselves, repent, ask forgiveness, and God forgives and forgets it ever happened. We must get to the point, by faith, where we do the same.

Do you believe that? Or do you think you must do some good works before you can get back into fellowship with God again? Will you ask forgiveness, receive His forgiveness by faith, and immediately come to the throne of grace to do as Hebrews 4:16 (AMP) says?

> *Let us then fearlessly and confidently and boldly draw*
> *near to the throne of grace (the throne of God's unmer-*
> *ited favor to us sinners), that we may receive mercy*
> *[for our failures] and find grace to help in good time*
> *for every need [appropriate help and well-timed help,*
> *coming just when we need it].*

Grace is not a one-time thing; we are to continually receive it. This may have been what God was telling Paul, to continually call on God's grace to combat the thorn in his flesh. According to James 4:6 (AMP), God is continually giving us grace: "But He gives us more and more grace (power of the Holy Spirit, to meet this evil tendency and all others fully). That is why He says, God sets Himself against the proud and haughty, but gives grace [continually] to the lowly (those who are humble enough to receive it)."

He continually gives grace (His unmerited favor) to those who are humble enough to receive it. What does this mean? It means those who recognize there is nothing they can do to earn His forgiveness. The proud would say, "I am keeping the Law. I am doing enough good to be blessed. I don't need to repent." They look to measure and compare; "I am better than so and so…" But the truth is it is impossible to earn God's favor. We just need to believe we have it. Know the truth, and the truth will set you free. Just as it is with all the things of God, as you continually press in, He will provide more and more revelation. Second Corinthians 8:9 (AMP) tells us this is so:

For you are becoming progressively acquainted with and recognizing more strongly and clearly the grace of our Lord Jesus Christ (His kindness, His gracious generosity, His undeserved favor and spiritual blessing), [in] that though He was [so very] rich, yet for your sakes He became [so very] poor, in order that by His poverty you might become enriched (abundantly supplied).

We need to continually remind ourselves that we are justified by grace, not by our works, and we need to continually let the enemy know that, as well. Think about that scripture from a business perspective. The Word of God is saying we will be abundantly supplied. How would knowing that God is always looking to abundantly supply us change your business planning and thinking? This is a very important point to consider. If we truly believe that God is our source, it allows us to take the focus off ourselves (meeting our needs and desires) and put the focus on the needs and desires of others. So many of our plans and decisions in business are based on managing around a perceived or an actual lack of something (a lack of understanding, a lack of investment dollars, a lack of available talent, etc.) rather than an abundance of something. This mindset can create some bad behaviors that can negatively impact our success.

In my career, I've been blessed to develop some innovative technical solutions and to manage some important relationships. Over the years, several of my team members and other leaders have come to me about developing a strategy to protect our solutions and our relationships from competitors. My answer has always been, "Why do I want to spend a lot of my time and energy trying to defend something we've already developed? I would rather spend most of our energy and investments continuing to innovate and expand our solutions and relationships." This approach has proven to deliver very positive results for me over the years.

One approach is fear-based, and the other is trusting in the Word of God and believing He wants us to continue to increase. This is one of the keys to the success I have experienced in my career. This is only because I can confidently stand on His Word purely because of His gift of grace to me, and I don't have to wonder if I deserve it and if the promises in God's Word are for me.

All of us must make daily decisions about how we spend our time and energy. I could choose to spend some of my limited time and energy defending what I have won, or I could spend the time and energy continuing to grow innovative thinking and influence (moving forward). One approach is fear-based, and one is faith-based, faith in God's grace toward me and His desire for my success. Despite what others are saying around me, I can take the faith approach, and I will have the favor and the spiritual blessing to be abundantly supplied with the talent I need around me, the financial resources I need, and the wisdom I need to leverage both to provide innovative solutions and grow relationships. I believe that because I know God's favor is on me, not because I am a *good person* and deserve it, but because I choose to believe the Word, which says:

> *Even when we were dead (slain) by [our own] short-comings and trespasses, He made us alive together in fellowship and in union with Christ; [He gave us the very life of Christ Himself, the same new life with which He quickened Him, for] it is by grace (His favor and mercy which you did not deserve) that you are saved (delivered from judgment and made partakers of Christ's salvation).*
>
> Ephesians 2:5 (AMP)

> *[And He did it in order] that we might be justified by His grace (by His favor, wholly undeserved), [that we might be acknowledged and counted as conformed to the divine will in purpose, thought, and action], and that we might become heirs of eternal life according to [our] hope.*
>
> Titus 3:7 (AMP)

Scripture tells us we are in right standing with God and that God's favor is constantly on us. Do we dare to believe it? Will you believe that God's favor is on you when you go into the next big meeting? Will you believe that when you present your ideas or go after a new piece of business, God's favor is upon you, independent of what you did yesterday or this morning? Will you dare to believe and walk in the freedom that God's grace provides? This means you never have to condemn yourself again. Will you use your faith to believe that now?

As I mentioned earlier, the Bible says we must judge our actions. It does not tell us to condemn ourselves for these actions. The question we need to ask ourselves is, "Will I allow God's grace to change my view of myself? Is my faith developed to the point where I see myself as righteous in God's eyes and believe that all of His promises are for me?"

Satan doesn't want me to believe it. He wants me to continue to feel the guilt. He wants me to keep my focus on myself and believe I can earn God's favor and then work like a dog only so that he can remind me again about my latest sin and tell me I've still not hit the mark. He wants me to think that neither God nor His favor are with me in the meeting today because of the argument I had with my wife this morning. No matter what we do, Satan will let us know that anything we do to try to earn God's favor is not enough, and he will point out the next thing we need to do to be worthy. He uses this mindset to keep us in bondage, which leads to many other sins:

- I become proud and judgmental because I compare my works with others. This is how I know I am working harder to be righteous than others; therefore, I am better than they are.
- My heart becomes hard, and I don't extend grace to others because I don't think they are working as hard as I am to obtain right standing with God. So, they don't deserve it until they work as hard or harder at it than I do.
- I work myself to exhaustion to keep the scoreboard in my favor. The enemy will cause us to focus our energy and efforts on doing good works

Business as a Calling | Derick Masengale

instead of on the truth in the Word and building our faith and our relationship with God.

"But Derick, you're implying there are no consequences for our sins." First, it is not my point of view or opinion; it is what the Bible says. If we are faithful to humble ourselves, to repent and confess our sins, God is faithful to forgive our sins, and we are immediately back in right standing with Him. Second, I did not say there were no consequences of sin. I did say that sin no longer breaks our relationship with God when we confess it to Him. No sin we commit can break that relationship with Him once we accept Jesus' sacrifice on the cross and are born again. However, when we sin, it most certainly impacts our everyday lives and our relationships with those around us.

For example, what can gossip do to your friendships? What does committing adultery do to your marriage? What does abusing alcohol or drugs do to your health, your ability to hold a job, and your ability to maintain your relationships with family and friends? What does lying to a co-worker do to your influence in the organization? Sin is of the devil. Nothing good comes from it, and we need to resist it. But thank God, when we mess up, we can confess our sins and immediately be in right standing with God. It may take a lot longer, however, to repair the relationship damage our sins created.

Without a revelation of grace, my focus is completely on me and what I do. I become selfish and self-centered. I need to try to keep racking up points on the good side of the scoreboard, but even when I do good, my motivation is focused on what's in it for me, not what's in it for others or out of love for God. I am doing the good works so I can earn something for me. It is impossible to walk in love and love others when my focus is on me. This is one of the biggest challenges for those of us who are operating in the business world.

How different would we operate if our focus was not on us? Would our impact be greater? As we analyze our network of relationships, we can quickly recognize those who are primarily focused on themselves, and we can see the results of the decisions that are based on self-interest. We can't blame those who make those types of decisions because if they don't have the Word and an understanding of how God desires us to operate, they have very little else to base their decisions on—at best, some organizational ethics policy. However, those policies only work if the fear of losing your job by getting caught violating the policy outweighs the fear of not operating in self-interest.

Christians can do the same thing but for different reasons and produce less-than-desired results. We can focus on ourselves and view ourselves as unworthy and flawed; after all, the scoreboard tells us we are unworthy, and we can even let the enemy convince us we are being humble by doing so. Yes, the enemy can deceive us into believing we are being humble even when our focus is completely on self. This self-centered view leads to weak and fearful followers of Christ.

We can become people who don't feel we deserve success in our professional or personal lives. We don't think we can take on a role of more responsibility, can make key decisions, or believe that God will help us in any of those situations. This self-centered view creates an interesting dynamic. Many in the world are striving to take more power, more money, and more of the agenda so they can validate themselves, while Christians are afraid to step out and strive for power, for money, and for the agenda because they don't think they are worthy of having them, or they think those things are ungodly. They are spending their time trying to rack up points on the good-works side of the scoreboard so they can become worthy of it. Both behaviors are a result of a self-centered view, and a primary tactic of the enemy is to keep our eyes focused on ourselves and not on Jesus. The Word of God tells me that God wants His people in positions of power and wealth to support spreading the good news of the gospel—grace.

I have seen this in my life. The enemy will do anything he can to get me to focus on me and not on God or others. I have learned that above all, I must focus on what Jesus did on the cross and the grace He gave me to put me in right standing with God and open the doors of heaven for His blessings. I want to close this chapter with the following scripture:

> *For if because of one man's trespass (lapse, offense) death reigned through that one, much more surely will those who receive [God's] overflowing grace (unmerited favor) and the free gift of righteousness [putting them into right standing with Himself] reign as kings in life through the one Man Jesus Christ (the Messiah, the Anointed One).*
>
> Romans 5:17 (AMP)

When we receive God's grace, we receive His gift of righteousness. It is a gift; it is not earned. By receiving it, all of His promises are made available to us, and we reign as kings in life (a position of power). When we reign as kings, the devil does not. When we reign as kings, sin does not. When we reign as kings, we are able to impact the world for Jesus and bless those around us. I encourage you to take a couple of weeks, go through the book of Proverbs, and underline all the scriptures that refer to the righteous or to righteousness. Study them to see what God has promised the righteous, and then consider what that means to you as you operate daily in your profession. It will provide you with a picture of how God wants us to reign in roles within the business community.

Above all, never again let the devil steal your blessings or influence by accepting his narrative about how unrighteous and undeserving you are. Remind him that you have the righteousness of Christ, and you don't need to do anything to keep it other than to believe. God wants you to be successful, not primarily for you, but so you can impact as many people as possible for His kingdom by extending grace and love to them.

Applying the Fundamentals and Delivering Impact

CHAPTER 6

Operating in Faith—
Sowing the Word

The sower sows the Word. And it will produce 30, 60 or 100 fold.

Mark 4:14 (AMP)

In this chapter, I want to take the principles presented in chapter three and discuss how to apply them to the daily challenges we face in our vocations. As I noted earlier, it is incumbent upon us to be knowledgeable of the Word, speak the Word in faith, and expect the sown Word (the Word we speak and confess) to produce results in our lives. We studied the parable of the sower and the seed in Mark 4.

And He said, "The kingdom of God is like a man who scatters seed upon the ground, And then continues sleeping and rising night and day while the seed sprouts and grows and increases—he knows not how."

Mark 4:26–27 (AMP)

We sow the Word, and God provides the increase. What is that increase?

The sower sows the Word. And it will produce 30, 60 or 100 fold. […] but when they hear, Satan comes at once and [by force] takes away the message which is sown in them.

Mark 4:14 (AMP)

Thirty, sixty, or one hundred times that which was sown. Sowing seeds for physical healing, spiritual growth, or financial increase, for example, produces thirty, sixty, or one hundred times that which was sown. How do we sow the Word? We find the verses in Scripture that provide God's promises in an area we need help in ("I have a physical challenge"; "I need a financial increase"; "I need to become a more effective leader"), and we confess (sow) them. Scripture tells us that as we confess the Word, our faith increases: "faith comes by hearing and hearing by the Word of God."

However, the scripture also tells us that Satan comes immediately to take away the Word that was sown—to steal our faith. How does Satan come to take away the Word? By getting us to change our confession and increase our faith in something other than the Word of God. He uses five main tactics to steal the Word out of our hearts and mouths and make it unfruitful in our lives. Mark 4:19 (AMP) outlines these techniques:

- Affliction: Satan comes against us physically to weaken our strength and resolve for standing on the Word.
- Persecution: Satan uses people (some of whom are very important to us) to attack us and criticize the things we are believing in.

- Cares of the world: Satan uses fear to convince us we are making a poor choice by standing on the Word and that we will fail because of it.
- Deceitfulness of riches: Satan tells us the riches of the world are the most important things to strive for because they will provide us happiness. If we want to obtain them, then our focus has to be on that pursuit.
- The lust for other things: Satan gives us a constant desire for more so that we spend time pursuing the things of this world and not the things of God.

The enemy is cunning; he has been deceiving people for centuries, and he knows how to use thoughts, people, and circumstances to get us off track in at least one of these areas. He will do it little by little until we look up at some point and wonder how we got so far off track. The enemy may be cunning, but he is powerless to stop us from obtaining God's best. We must decide not to allow one or all of the tactics described above to distract us from trusting in God's Word.

Satan cannot force us to do anything. He can apply a lot of pressure, but we have the freedom to decide which path we will walk in every situation. The Bible says, "he comes as a roaring lion seeking whom he may devour," but for followers of Christ, he is all roar and no bite. He has no power over us. He can get a hold in our lives only if we let him, and the first step to stopping him is knowing the Word. Mark 4:19 tells us how he is going to try to gain a foothold in our lives. James 4:7 tells us to resist the devil, and he will flee from us.

With that understanding, we can recognize when the enemy is creeping in with one of these tactics and trying to steal our faith. He is trying to steal the faith we have in the promises of God that we sowed by speaking the Word. I would suggest that all of these tactics are based on fear. Fear is the opposite of faith. For a follower of Christ, fear says, "Maybe God's promises are true, but they may not be true for me. I'm not sure God will take care of me and that He meant all of His promises for me." I spend an entire chapter later in this book talking about how fear impacts success in every area of our lives.

If Satan can get us to doubt God's promises, then his next step is to produce thoughts of fear in a given area. Often, we give the enemy an opening by entertaining doubt. Doubt, if you get to its base, is a fear that "God does not love me because I am not righteous enough, and therefore He will not bless me as the Word says." As we learned in the last chapter, that is a lie. We have His grace and, therefore, His righteousness. To be clear, when I say prosper, I am not talking just about money. God's prosperity touches all areas of our lives:

- Spiritually
- Financially
- Emotionally
- Physically
- Relationally

Proverbs 10:22 says His blessings come with no sorrow. That means I can have financial prosperity and be in good health. It means I can have success in my career and not lose my family and damage relationships along the way. How do we remove the doubt that God will do what He says He will do for us? We remove the doubt and block Satan's attack by meditating on and hearing God's Word to build our faith and then acting on what we hear. The Bible refers to our faith as our shield by which we quench all the flaming missiles of the enemy (Ephesians 6:16). We can use our faith in God and His Word to rebuke the enemy every time we find him coming at us with affliction, persecution, cares of this world, deceitfulness of riches, and the lust for other things. We must remain aware and diligent and use the shield of faith to put down thoughts (the enemy's flaming darts) that conflict with the promises of God.

"That's all well and good, Derick, but I don't know if I have any faith," or "I have faith, but it doesn't seem as though it is enough to change my circumstances. I need more faith." Romans 10:17 (KJV) provides a key to increasing our faith: "So then faith cometh by hearing, and hearing by the word of God."

How do you increase your faith? By hearing and studying the Word of God. It is vitally important to keep the Word of God in the forefront of our mind and in the forefront of the way we talk about our situations. If we do, it is much more difficult for the enemy to come and steal the faith we have in God's promises and His faithfulness to see them come to pass in our lives. As we gain little victories along the way, it becomes much easier to believe God for the next thing. Walking by faith takes practice and time, just like any other endeavor. If you want to be good at it, you must work at it. Start your faith "workout," and give God an opportunity to show His faithfulness to His promises.

The more our focus is on God and His purpose for our lives, the more difficult it is for the enemy to distract us from the destiny God has planned for us.

Why is this relevant to the business world and our vocations? Let me ask you a few questions:

- Do you need faith to perform your job? Do you believe God has placed you in or led you to that role? If He has, then from experience, I can safely say that you do. God puts us in positions that require skill, experience, and knowledge that we don't fully possess, and as a result, we must trust Him to help us develop and successfully operate in the role.

- If you believe God has put you there, do you expect to prosper in all you do? God's Word says we should expect to be successful wherever God places us. We need to rely on our faith, the Holy Spirit, and the Word sown to carry us through the times when it looks as though success will not happen.

- Do you expect God's favor to be on you? God's Word says to expect it. He says He will exalt us. We need to take that by faith, or we will try to exalt ourselves. If we achieve something based on our own strength, then it will require our strength to keep us there. If God places us there, then He makes available all we need to be successful in that place. We can rely on His strength and not just our own. Most importantly, if we trust that God will exalt us in His time, then we can focus on blessing others and not focus on our situation constantly.

- Do you believe that God has anointed (empowered you) to perform your job? God's Word says He has. It is God's will that we prosper in all we do, which means in all we do that aligns with His will. If He led you to your current position, then it is His will for you to prosper in that position no matter what the circumstances may say.

Knowing God's Word and knowing that you are in God's plan for your life makes you a very powerful member in the body of Christ and very dangerous to the enemy. It is extremely important not to lose your focus on God's Word. Remember what we discussed in chapter three; Mark 4:24 (AMP) says: "And He said to them, Be careful what you are hearing. The measure [of thought and study] you give [to the truth you hear] will be the measure [of virtue and knowledge] that comes back to you— and more [besides] will be given to you who hear."

So how do you increase your faith? By hearing and measuring what you hear. One of the primary ways to hear is to confess those scriptures that speak to your challenge. For many of us, every day, we must face a never-ending chain of decisions and challenges in the workplace and at home. The things you hear coming out of your mouth in pressure situations measure where you are on the scale of faith vs. fear and doubt.

> *"O generation of vipers, how can ye, being evil, speak good things? for out of the abundance of the heart the mouth speaketh."*
>
> Matthew 12:34 (KJV)

I try to pay close attention to the words that are coming out of me, and if I hear words of fear or words that contradict what God says, I know I am drifting from the truth, and I am providing the enemy an opportunity to come in, choke the Word,

Are you speaking words that are declaring your own failure in the workplace?

and steal my blessing. To address it, I need to go back to filling my ears and my spirit with the Word of God. Are you speaking words that are declaring your own failure in the workplace? Do you continually talk about all the challenges and difficulties, or are you more focused on God's promises and solutions? If the enemy can get you to confess, "I'm not worthy of this," or "I'm not smart enough to do this," or "Things are never going to change," he is using your words to steal your thirty-, sixty-, or one-hundred-fold return. Some see these confessions as a form of humility; that is a lie! True humility is recognizing we can't reach true success by our efforts alone and that it is God who gets us there. It is based not only on our skills, talent, and hard work, but it is also God's blessings on each of those to produce true and lasting success.

I want faith-filled words to be the norm coming out of me; it is so important in the workplace. So much of the business world, by nature, is negative. I often find myself in very negative situations, and if I am not careful, I can let the negative culture begin to seep in and affect what I think and say. God has given us His Word and instructed us to speak (sow) it in faith as we are led by the Holy Spirit to change the circumstances around us. He has told us that it is how His kingdom operates. There is a power in speaking God's Word in faith. God showed us in the first book of the Bible how His kingdom operates. God created the heavens and the earth by speaking faith-filled words. In Genesis 1:2–7 (AMP):

> *The earth was without form and an empty waste, and darkness was upon the face of the very great deep. The Spirit of God was moving (hovering, brooding) over the face of the waters. And God said, Let there be light; and there was light. And God saw that the light was good (suitable, pleasant) and He approved it; and God separated the light from the darkness. And God called the light Day, and the darkness He called Night. And there was evening and there was morning, one day.*

God created the universe and all living things through faith-filled words. His Holy Spirit was moving over the face of the earth just waiting for a command or word from the Father. God spoke, and the Holy Spirit responded by releasing His power to make the words come to pass. Nothing happened in Scripture without God speaking His

God's Word combined with faith calls on the Holy Spirit to change the environment around you.

Word or having one of His prophets or angels speak the Word for Him. God's Word combined with faith calls on the Holy Spirit to change the environment around us. If you are speaking God's Word by faith, you are speaking hope and providing a positive outlook to those around you.

I am not talking about standing up in a boardroom and quoting scripture or saying, "Thus sayeth the Lord God." I am saying we should not be spreading the negativity by repeating what others may be saying that contradicts God's promises to us.

We should, however, be praying God's will into the environment and releasing the power of the Holy Spirit. How do we do that? By confessing His Word in prayer. The fruit of that in your life will allow you to be the one who has a positive attitude and an expectation that things can and will be better, independent of what the current circumstances say. Others will notice and look to you in times of difficulty for encouragement. This is not just a spiritual truth. There is a very practical side to this, as well.

As I assemble teams, I am always looking for those who have a positive outlook to help me tackle a challenge. I don't want negative people as key members of my team. They may not realize it, but I know their words will weaken the team. I want team members who believe the goal can be accomplished and encourage one another to meet the challenge no matter how daunting it may be.

The passage from Genesis above demonstrates how God's words have the power to create. We have the same opportunity, and I believe the mandate from God to use our faith in God's Word to create as we discussed previously:

1. Goods and services that will allow a community to flourish
2. Opportunities for employees to express at least a portion of their God-given identity through meaningful, creative work

As believers, we need to recognize that God has given us His Word to sow and take authority over our circumstances so we can align them with the plan of God. Let me provide a biblical example of speaking the Word to take authority in a situation.

In Matthew 4, we find Satan tempting Jesus in the wilderness. Matthew 4:1–3 (AMP):

> *Then Jesus was led (guided) by the [Holy] Spirit into the wilderness (desert) to be tempted (tested and tried) by the devil. And He went without food for forty days and forty nights, and later He was hungry. And the tempter came and said to Him, If You are God's Son, command these stones to be made [loaves of] bread.*

This is one of the enemy's shrewd tests. He doesn't know if Jesus is the Son of God, so he is trying to get Him to tell him. Remember what the Bible says: if the people had known who He was, they never would have crucified the Lord of glory. Also, look at the test itself: Jesus had been fasting, and the devil came at Him with the cares of this world. "You need to eat something; you should address the needs of your body." Matthew 4:4–7 (AMP):

> *But He replied, It has been written, Man shall not live and be upheld and sustained by bread alone, but by every word that comes forth from the mouth of God. Then the devil took Him into the holy city and placed Him on a turret (pinnacle, gable) of the temple sanctuary. And he said to Him, If You are the Son of God, throw Yourself down; for it is written, He will give His angels charge over you, and they will bear you up on their hands, lest you strike your foot against a stone. Jesus said to him, On the other hand, it is written also, You shall not tempt, test thoroughly, or try exceedingly the Lord your God.*

Jesus used the Word against the devil, and the devil tried to trick Jesus by misquoting Scripture. This test was a form of persecution, and Satan threw in the tried-and-true test of pride to try to trip up Jesus. "If you are the Son of God, prove it!" Again, Jesus shut him down using the Word. Finally, in Matthew 4:8–11 (AMP):

> *Again, the devil took Him up on a very high mountain and showed Him all the kingdoms of the world and the glory (the splendor, magnificence, preeminence, and excellence) of them. And he said to Him, These things, all taken together, I will give You, if You will prostrate Yourself before me and do homage and worship me. Then Jesus said to him, Begone, Satan! For it has been written, You shall worship the Lord your God, and Him alone shall you serve. Then the devil departed from Him, and behold, angels came and ministered to Him.*

Here, the devil came at Jesus with the deceitfulness of riches and lust for other things. Again, Jesus shut him down with the Word and then told him to go. Then God sent His angels to minister to Him.

The passages above demonstrate how to use the Word (the sword of the Spirit) to take authority over the attacks and situations that are not aligning with the will of God. Jesus Himself had to use the Word to take authority over the enemy, and He had to do it more than once! He had to continue to use the Word on the enemy until he departed (resist and he will flee). God has given us His Word and His Spirit to prompt us in the use of the Word. Are you taking authority over situations around you that are not aligned with the Word and will of God? How do you do it?

- Step one is to know the Word of God. We can't rebuke the enemy if we don't know what God's will is for that situation or circumstance we are faced with.
- Step two is to sow the Word. We must decide if we are going to use the Word. We decide whose report we are going to believe; God's promises or Satan's lies.
- Step three is having done all to stand, stand. Once you know God's will and you have sown God's Word, stand in faith until the situation changes. In the example above, even Jesus had to stand. He had to stand against the devil three times before He left.
- Step four is standing for complete victory. Don't stop standing when you see some results. Stand until everything you are sowing for comes to pass. Remember it is the measure you mete. Don't settle for less than God's best.

In my professional career, I have had to apply these principles many times. There was a period in my career when I was sent in succession to multiple clients to resurrect failing programs. Those are very difficult situations because trust has broken down across the stakeholders, and team morale is very low within the client and contractor organizations. In many cases, the team's and the client's outlook had become very negative. Depending on the size of the challenge, it can take many months or more than a year to right the ship. But it always started with believing it was God's purpose for me to be there, sowing God's Word in prayer for a good outcome, and staying in the Word so I could provide a positive attitude to the team and remain open to any idea that would help change the situation. In every instance, we were able to turn the troubled program around for our clients. I know that my focus on walking by these principles was a key reason I was able to keep a positive outlook, continually encourage the team, and provide confidence to the clients during very difficult circumstances.

I don't say that to diminish the hard work provided by each team member. Their collective effort was fundamental to the ultimate success, and without their commitment and effort, success would have been impossible. But I will say the effort alone is not enough. The team was working really hard when things were going south before I got there. God placed me there and provided the wisdom and grace I needed to help lead the team forward. I made mistakes, but God's promises didn't change, and it was His desire to make the project a success. As I continued to practice walking in faith, I got better at hearing Him and following His leading in each subsequent assignment.

As a leader, what you believe and what you say affects the entire team. Some lead by bringing fear and strife, and others lead by bringing hope, encouragement, and peace. Which environment would you rather work in? Which one is more conducive to lasting success? I can say from experience that it is not easy to bring hope and peace to a failing environment. It is easy to be consumed by all the negativity and the pressure to produce. It is easy to make excuses for missed commitments and blame others for all the problems. But God's Word tells us to expect a different outcome. If we stand on His Word in faith, we can begin to change that environment little by little. It is not easy, it takes hard work on the jobsite, and it takes effort to continue to stand on God's promises in prayer. If we do those things, however, God will use us to turn difficult situations around. I know it; I have experienced it. If He has done it for me, He will do it for you. The Bible tells us that God is no respecter of persons.

As discussed, a fundamental key to success is what we say in tough situations. This brings me to the next topic I want to touch on here, the power of the tongue.

> *Death and life are in the power of the tongue, and they who indulge in it shall eat the fruit of it [for death or life].*
>
> Proverbs 18:21 (AMP)

> *For Jerusalem is ruined and Judah is fallen, because their speech and their deeds are against the Lord, to provoke the eyes of His glory and defy His glorious presence.*
>
> Isaiah 3:8 (AMP)

This is so important to your personal success, witness, and the success of your business and team:

- Are you destroying your future with your own words?
- Are your words negatively impacting the performance of your teams?
- Are your words negatively impacting your influence and the success of your career?

I have found the devil is always trying to put pressure on us to speak crosswise with the Word of God. He often does it through other people. They will come to you under great pressure and try to push that pressure onto you. They will declare the sky is falling and want you to become as anxious as they are about the situation (remember the apostles in the boat when they woke Jesus). If you don't, they don't believe you care about or understand the issue. I can't tell you how many times I have heard someone say, "You don't seem to have a sense of urgency about this." Translation: "Unless you are as worked up as I am about the situation, you are not giving it the emphasis required."

In these types of situations, if I don't have an immediate answer, I have learned to say nothing or say "I don't know" rather than get pulled into that strife—the cares of this world. It is rare that a critical decision needs to be made in the moment. I will listen, make sure I understand the issue, and tell them I will get back to them. I will take it before the Lord in prayer and seek His guidance. My visible anxiety about a situation is not the measure of how committed I am to address the problem at hand. I am as committed as my co-workers; my approach is just different.

This approach will always produce two very practical outcomes: (1) the added time will allow much of the emotion to be removed from the situation so that it is easier to assess what the real issue is and hear from God, and (2) it allows more time to assess how much fear is impacting the situation and driving the need for a decision. I have dedicated a whole chapter of this book to recognizing and combating fear, but I will briefly touch on it here.

Much of the pressure we face is based on the issues others bring to us. Many of those issues are based on fear, such as the fear of not meeting a deadline or the fear of making a wrong decision and wanting someone else to make it. Or someone won't share information because they fear they are giving up ownership and reducing their value in the organization if they share their knowledge. These examples are common across large teams and always lead to significant strife within the team or organization.

I have learned that addressing fear and the strife that accompanies it is one of the most important things we can do in these types of situations. We use prayer, the Word of God, and the Holy Spirit to help us know how to do it. If you are praying the Word of God, you are praying His will, and He declares it will go forth and do what He has purposed it to do. So, find verses in the Bible that relate to the challenge you are facing and begin to confess them in prayer. I have found that sowing and reaping the Word (by faith) is one of the two main ways to operate in God's will and power.

So, find verses in the Bible that relate to the challenge you are facing and begin to confess them in prayer.

God wanted me to be successful in every one of those situations He sent me to clean up. The success was not for me per se but to help the struggling team gel as a team and get the satisfaction of working together to deliver a good product. The success was also for the client, who was depending on the good product to improve their business or mission. During these situations, I have also found that the Word of God does not have all the answers I need for each decision I need to make daily, for example:

- If I have two conflicting accounts about a situation, which one is accurate?

- If there are twenty issues to address, which is the most important?
- What is the real issue causing challenges for my team, and what is just a symptom of the real issue?

So, when you can't find a specific answer in the Word, how do you know God's will? As shared in a previous chapter, thank God that He has sent His Holy Spirit to guide us in making these decisions. John 14:26 (AMP) states:

> But the Comforter (Counselor, Helper, Intercessor, Advocate, Strengthener, Standby), the Holy Spirit, Whom the Father will send in My name [in My place, to represent Me and act on My behalf], He will teach you all things. And He will cause you to recall (will remind you of, bring to your remembrance) everything I have told you.

We will spend time in the next chapter learning how to allow the Holy Spirit to provide insight and God's wisdom to the decisions we must make daily.

CHAPTER 7

Operating in the Power of the Holy Spirit

But you shall receive power (ability, efficiency, and might) when the Holy Spirit has come upon you, and you shall be My witnesses in Jerusalem and all Judea and Samaria and to the ends (the very bounds) of the earth.

Acts 1:8 (AMP)

In chapter four, we talked about the Holy Spirit: who He is, why He was sent, and how we receive Him. Before we dive into how to fellowship with the Holy Spirit, I want to reiterate that God wants to speak to each of us, and the number one way He does that is through His Word. In Hosea 4:6 (AMP), the Word of God says, "My people are destroyed for a lack of knowledge"—a lack of knowledge of His Word. As we have discussed, it is incumbent upon us to study His Word and to sow His Word. But how do you know what God's will is when you need to make a decision that is not covered in the Word? We discussed previously how God sent His Holy Spirit to be our counselor and helper in those situations. As a reminder, let's look at 1 Corinthians 2:10–13 (AMP):

Yet to us God has unveiled and revealed them by and through His Spirit, for the [Holy] Spirit searches

*diligently, exploring and examining everything, even
sounding the profound and bottomless things of God
[the divine counsels and things hidden and beyond
man's scrutiny]. For what person perceives (knows and
understands) what passes through a man's thoughts
except the man's own spirit within him? Just so no one
discerns (comes to know and comprehend) the thoughts
of God except the Spirit of God. Now we have not
received the spirit [that belongs to] the world, but the
[Holy] Spirit Who is from God, [given to us] that we
might realize and comprehend and appreciate the gifts
[of divine favor and blessing so freely and lavishly]
bestowed on us by God. And we are setting these truths
forth in words not taught by human wisdom but
taught by the [Holy] Spirit, combining and interpreting spiritual truths with spiritual language [to those
who possess the Holy Spirit].*

In summary, the spirit of God knows the thoughts of God.
God has given us the Holy Spirit to know the gifts He has
bestowed upon us. These gifts minister to all areas of our being:
body, soul, and spirit. They could manifest as a financial blessing
to take care of our physical needs, a strong mind and the right
desires to help meet our emotional needs, and spiritual gifts to
help us release God's wisdom and love to those around us.

The scripture tells us when you hear from the Holy Spirit,
you will know God's thoughts and His will for a situation, any
situation. What an amazing promise. We receive and manifest
God's promises in our lives by faith. In this chapter, I want to
examine how to develop and walk in a deeper relationship with
the Holy Spirit. Let's start by looking at John 16:13 (AMP):

But when He, the Spirit of Truth (the Truth-giving Spirit) comes, He will guide you into all the Truth (the whole, full Truth). For He will not speak His own message [on His own authority]; but He will tell whatever He hears [from the Father; He will give the message that has been given to Him], and He will announce and declare to you the things that are to come [that will happen in the future].

This verse clearly says that God will lead us into all truth. Do you think this would be valuable in determining which decision to resolve a conflict or to bring clarity to a highly ambiguous situation? We have learned that God has given the Holy Spirit to all those who follow Christ. We also need to continually remind ourselves that the Holy Spirit is our Comforter (Counselor, Helper, Intercessor, Advocate, Strengthener, and Standby). His willingness to play any, and all, of those roles is not based on anything we've done. It is based on the work of the cross done through the death and resurrection of Jesus and His love for us. We must believe that we can call on God and know that the Holy Spirit will respond to us in our time of need. This is so important for how we live our lives, which includes how we operate in our vocation. If we could hear the Holy Spirit's thoughts about a decision or situation we are facing at work and act on them, we would never make a wrong decision.

"I can't believe that, Derick. We won't ever make a wrong decision? That's unbelievable." That is what the Bible says. Remember it is the measure you mete. In addition to believing this promise, our challenge is to develop our ability to hear God speaking to us in all situations through His Holy Spirit. We must give the Holy Spirit space in our lives to speak to us, and we must develop our ability to perceive and recognize His leading, no matter how great the turmoil swirling around us is. The Holy Spirit is a gentleman. He is never going to be the loudest voice you hear. We must learn to discern the difference between what we are sensing in our spirit and what we are hearing in our soul (mind, will, and emotions) and put the spirit first.

How valuable do you think this would make you to your employer, clients, or customers you serve? As we have seen, it was very valuable to the kings that Daniel and Joseph served. It is a huge differentiator that we as Christians have and that sadly so few walk in. The business world actually recognizes the fruit of the Holy Spirit, but they don't know what to attribute it to. If you continually make good decisions, some view that as a measure of intelligence. Others may view it as wisdom, and still, others may view it as being skillful.

I was in a corporate leadership class where we were examining what I thought was a fascinating research study, entitled "Level 5 Leadership: The Triumph of Humility and Great Resolve," published by Jim Collins in the *Harvard Business Review*. His research team conducted a five-year study to see why some companies succeeded and others didn't. As one might expect, they were looking to see if they could find common principles for organizations to operate by to increase success, in other words, dos and don'ts for corporate success. Out of the 1,435 Fortune 500 companies that Collins studied, only eleven achieved and sustained greatness, which his team defined as garnering stock returns at least three times what the market returned for fifteen years after a major transition period. What did these eleven companies have in common? Each had what the research team termed a "Level 5" leader at the helm. Collins stated, "Level 5 refers to the highest level in a hierarchy of executive capabilities that we identified during our research. Leaders at the other four levels in the hierarchy can produce high degrees of success but not enough to elevate companies from mediocrity to sustained excellence."[4]

What are the attributes of a Level 5 leader? According to Collins, Level 5 leaders blend the paradoxical combination of deep, personal humility with intense professional will. Based on what we have studied to this point, isn't this what the Word teaches us? Certainly, one aspect of a professional will is becoming skillful and diligent about our craft. A second aspect would be a commitment and passion to produce high-quality products and services that bless our communities and operate the business in a fashion that also provides opportunities to leverage employee talents and experience. It is not just about our personal success. I provided the scriptural basis for this in a previous chapter.

How can a follower of Christ not be humble? If you truly believe that Jesus is leading you in your career by providing you opportunities and the wisdom to be successful, then you know you are not in those roles because of your skill alone. This also is a reason the enemy would like us not to see our profession as God-ordained. If we think we are driving our success, then it is virtually impossible to walk in humility. Without the realization that lasting success is tied to our relationship with God and His blessings on us (true humility), it will not be possible to reach the level of success that God desires for us or the level of success Collins identified in his research. This is what the Word teaches and not coincidently what the researchers found.

It was interesting that when Collins and his team started to look at what drove the sustained excellence, they originally didn't want to put much emphasis on the leader, but the data led them to find they could not escape the fact that the leader was the key to achieving the success of the organization.

He goes on to say, "My preliminary hypothesis is that there are two categories of people: those who don't have the Level 5 seed within them and those who do." Very interesting that he used the term "seed." Collins suggests there is something about these leaders, which he calls a "seed," that is not tied to their education, their network, or their experience that separates them from other leaders. He also found that "leaders without the seed tend to have monumental egos they can't subjugate to something larger and more sustaining than themselves" (i.e., their companies). Or in our case, God and His reasons for creating business:

1. Provide goods and services that will allow a community to flourish
2. Serve employees by providing them with opportunities to express at least a portion of their God-given identity through meaningful, creative work

Collins identified a seed, but his team could not determine why individuals had it or exactly what it was. And even though he did spend a portion of the article talking about the development of the seed, his team could not provide the key to the inner development of the person who became a Level 5 leader.

I found this study fascinating and exciting. Based on my study of the Scriptures as well as my experience, I believe the seed to be the Holy Spirit. I'm not sure that one can reach a continued state of humility without knowledge of God's Word and a relationship with the Holy Spirit. God's Word says that He resists the proud. You want help from God? Then the first thing you need to do is humble yourself and ask for that help. This starts by asking

Jesus to forgive your sins and be the Lord of your life. Those who refuse to admit they don't have all the answers in public won't get answers from God in private. Humility is fundamental to receiving anything from God. This research team deduced that the leader's humility was a key to leading an organization to a high level of success.

This is a clear example of how God uses His children in business to bless communities and employees in a manner that others can't. Don't misunderstand me; non-Christians can be successful in business, as well, but there is a limit to their success and impact. Collins stated what prevented the Level 4 leaders from reaching the next level was often their egos. They have a difficult time seeing the bigger purpose of their roles and choosing long-term success over immediate gratification. Because of that, they hit a ceiling, and they were not able to lead the organization to higher sustained levels of success.

Our success is not just measured by position or income. It also includes physical health, emotional health, and relational health. God's desire is for us to achieve success in all areas, and His Holy Spirit was sent to lead us into that kind of success. I know I am not capable of doing that on my own. I proved that early in my life. Anyone who thinks they can demonstrates the lack of humility required to achieve it.

As we walk with God and become more like Him, humility is a trait that we take on. Why? Because humility is based on love, and God is love. If we are continuing to grow in our relationship with God, then we are continuing to grow in love, and our decisions will not be based on just how they affect us. They will be based on how they affect our colleagues and our customers. We will discuss this in more detail in the last chapter of this book. As followers of Christ, we can subjugate our egos by spending time with God in the study of His Word and in prayer. It is hard for egos to become too inflated when we continuously put God first in our lives and recognize Him as the source of all good things as the Bible teaches.

A second example comes from *The 21 Irrefutable Laws of Leadership* by John Maxwell. In his book, Maxwell lists intuition as law 8. "Leaders see everything with a leadership bias, and as a result, they instinctively, almost automatically, know what to do."[5] He also says, "The best way to describe this bias is an ability to get a handle on intangible factors, understand them, and work with them to accomplish leadership goals." How does this align with what we have discussed about the Holy Spirit?

Here is how Maxwell summarizes his chapter on intuition: "Leadership is really more art than science. The principles of leadership are constant, but the application changes with every leader and every situation. That's why it requires intuition. Without it, you can get blindsided, and that's one of the worst things that can happen to a leader. If you want to lead long, you've got to obey the Law of Intuition." I would translate that to "obey the 'knowing' we have about a situation."

We have discussed how listening to the Holy Spirit provides that "knowing" from deep inside us. If we are seeking guidance continually from the Holy Spirit, the chances of us being blindsided by anything are low and tied to how well we discern His leading, not on whether God is speaking to us about it. God knows the future, and He will use the leading of His Holy Spirit to position us properly for it. That is why He wants to see us in positions of influence. When He positions us, and we follow Him, we can position those we have leadership or influence over for the future, as well.

The world recognizes there is something (a seed, intuition) that separates the success of leaders, but they don't understand where it comes from or how to tap into it. But we who follow Christ can, and it is His will for us to do so. Below is the example of Joseph. If you remember the account we read earlier, after Joseph interpreted Pharaoh's dream, Pharaoh placed him in a position of leadership and essentially controlled all the commerce in that area of the world. In Genesis 41:33–40 (AMP), we find:

> *So now let Pharaoh seek out and provide a man*
> *discreet, understanding, proficient, and wise and set*
> *him over the land of Egypt [as governor]. Let Pharaoh*
> *do this; then let him select and appoint officers over*
> *the land, and take one-fifth [of the produce] of the*
> *[whole] land of Egypt in the seven plenteous years*
> *[year by year]. And let them gather all the food of these*
> *good years that are coming and lay up grain under*
> *the direction and authority of Pharaoh, and let them*
> *retain food [in fortified granaries] in the cities. And*
> *that food shall be put in store for the country against*
> *the seven years of hunger and famine that are to come*
> *upon the land of Egypt, so that the land may not be*
> *ruined and cut off by the famine. And the plan seemed*
> *good in the eyes of Pharaoh and in the eyes of all his*
> *servants. And Pharaoh said to his servants, Can we*
> *find this man's equal, a man in whom is the spirit of*
> *God? And Pharaoh said to Joseph, Forasmuch as [your]*
> *God has shown you all this, there is nobody as intelli-*
> *gent and discreet and understanding and wise as you*
> *are. You shall have charge over my house, and all my*
> *people shall be governed according to your word [with*

reverence, submission, and obedience]. Only in matters of the throne will I be greater than you are.

This is a perfect example of God placing a person who was constantly seeking Him and walking in His ways in a position of influence to bless the community. Joseph controlled all the commerce for Egypt, which, at that time, was the most powerful nation in the world. God did not set Joseph up to bless only the Jews. Certainly, God placed him in that role to bless the Jews; however, in doing so, he blessed the entire nation of Egypt and the surrounding region. While God may not use us to bless an entire nation, He does want us to be a blessing in our sphere of influence. If we spend the time listening for His direction, He will provide us the wisdom required to be the blessing. So how do we "hear" the promptings and leading of the Holy Spirit so He can use us to bless those around us? Let's start by look looking at Romans 8:14–16 (AMP):

> *For all who are led by the Spirit of God are sons of God. For [the Spirit which] you have now received [is] not a spirit of slavery to put you once more in bondage to fear, but you have received the Spirit of adoption [the Spirit producing sonship] in [the bliss of] which we cry, Abba (Father)! Father! The Spirit Himself [thus] testifies together with our own spirit, [assuring us] that we are children of God.*

God is confirming His direction by having His Spirit, whom He sent to live in us, testify (bear witness) with our spirit. In 1 Kings 19:12 (AMP), we find He manifests Himself as a still, small voice: "And after the earthquake a fire, but the Lord was not in the fire; and after the fire [a sound of gentle stillness and] a still, small voice."

The scripture doesn't say God spoke in an audible voice or that He provided a vision. Those types of manifestations happen, but Scripture teaches that is not the norm. The norm for God to communicate with us is the Holy Spirit bearing witness with our spirit. God is a spirit; we are a spirit that lives in a body, and we have a soul made up of our mind, our will, and our emotions. To hear, we must spend quiet time with God. This is a time with no TVs or music blaring, no texting or reading emails, just time in prayer, reading His Word, and intentionally listening for God to speak.

Don't get discouraged if you don't hear something the first time, the second, the third, or…If you continue to seek Him, Scripture tells us you will hear Him. I often find the cares of this world trying to creep in and take away from my quiet time with God. As soon as I sit down, my mind will often start thinking of a hundred different things, and it is hard to focus on God. Don't let that discourage you. It will take some practice to be able to turn down all the shouting that is going on in your mind to focus on sensing your spirit. It is a continual battle for me. Setting aside a regular time to get quiet before the Lord is a must if we want to hear the leading of the Holy Spirit. We need to stay at it and be diligent.

In my experience, I will pray for insight or help in an area over a period of time, and I will be reading the Bible, and a thought, often unrelated to the text I am reading, will come into my mind, but it's tied directly to what I have been praying about, and I will say to myself, "That's it. That's the answer to what I have been praying about." Because I was not thinking about the topic, I know it wasn't something I thought of, so then I check my spirit to see if I have peace about it. If I do, then I move forward. If I get a check (a lack of peace), I do not.

As with any promise in the Word, we must first be aware of the promise, and then we must believe it before we will see it manifest in our lives. We must recognize and believe that God will talk with us and provide direction for any question we have. If we believe this, our biggest challenge becomes waiting and hearing. God will answer in His time, and we must not give up until we hear. This is my biggest hurdle. I want answers, and I want them now. Waiting in faith is not easy. I have found myself becoming impatient more than once and moving out before getting a clear step from the Lord. That always produces less than God's best in my life.

The presence of the Holy Spirit in us is the seed and the source of intuition mentioned above. This is so important and such a differentiator that even the world has recognized the importance of the "seed" and is on a quest to figure out how to bring this to bear for their benefit. They just don't recognize or know the source. What an advantage we have. We know it is God's will to guide us into all truth, so we need to "come boldly to the throne" and ask. Then we need to be sensitive as we listen, and Scripture provides insight into how we do that. Let's look at Acts and see how things changed after the baptism of the Holy Spirit.

> *And they drew lots [between the two], and the lot fell on Matthias; and he was added to and counted with the eleven apostles (special messengers).*
>
> Acts 1:26 (AMP)

And they were all filled (diffused throughout their
souls) with the Holy Spirit and began to speak in other
(different, foreign) languages (tongues), as the Spirit
kept giving them clear and loud expression [in each
tongue in appropriate words].

Acts 2:4 (AMP)

Before the release of the Holy Spirit in Acts 2:4, the leaders made important decisions by chance. In this case, they drew lots to decide who would replace Judas as an apostle. That's a pretty big decision to make by chance, but at the time, they didn't know a better way to differentiate between two qualified candidates. Even though they drew lots, I'm sure God was involved in the result. However, in Acts 2:4, they were filled with the Holy Spirit, and how they made key decisions from that point forward changed significantly. There are many examples in the subsequent chapters of Acts of the Holy Spirit directing the apostles and laypeople alike. Look at how they made a similar decision in Acts 13:2 (AMP): "While they were worshiping the Lord and fasting, the Holy Spirit said, Separate now for Me Barnabas and Saul for the work to which I have called them."

Here they were looking to identify leaders just like in Acts 3; however, they had been filled with the Holy Spirit, so they called on the Spirit to guide them. As a result, when they were fasting and praying (spending time in the presence of God), the Holy Spirit told them who to set aside for the work. I don't believe the Holy Spirit spoke in an audible voice. Each person sensed in his spirit that it was good to select Barnabas and Saul.

We have already learned that the Holy Spirit speaks to our spirit to provide the will of God. I would like to make another point here: the Holy Spirit spoke to all of them at the same time and provided the same answer—"they [plural] were worshiping the Lord and fasting." The Holy Spirit that is in me is the same Holy Spirit that is in you and any other person who has accepted Jesus as Lord and Savior. When He provides direction and truth about a situation, He is going to say the same thing to all who are listening. As I mentioned, being led by the Holy Spirit is a continual learning process, and no one is perfect at it. God is merciful. He knows our hearts, and He will help clean up any mistakes we make as we try to follow His leading.

The example in Acts 13 shows we can get quiet in prayer and hear the Holy Spirit. But we can also quench the Holy Spirit. First Thessalonians 5:19–21 (AMP) tells us:

> Do not quench (suppress or subdue) the [Holy] Spirit;
> Do not spurn the gifts and utterances of the prophets
> [do not depreciate prophetic revelations nor despise
> inspired instruction or exhortation or warning]. But
> test and prove all things [until you can recognize] what
> is good; [to that] hold fast.

So how do we do that? For starters, we can choose not to believe it. You can believe the Holy Spirit is not real and that He doesn't speak to God's people, and I can guarantee you won't hear Him speak to you. However, for those who are seeking to hear, remember the verse we studied in a previous chapter: "the cares of the world come in and choke the Word." We can find ourselves so busy that we don't spend any quiet time in prayer, seeking God's direction, the result of which is quenching the Holy Spirit.

It is not always our busyness that is quenching the Holy Spirit, however. The enemy will also try to apply pressure through others. This is very common in a business environment. How often have you seen individuals raise an issue and not feel they've done their jobs until they can make you as anxious about the problem as they are? It has happened to me many times, and if we are not careful in these situations, we can allow that pressure to cause us to focus on the problem and not get quiet before the Lord to hear the answer to the problem.

The enemy is constantly working to drown out the still, small voice by trying to prevent us from getting quiet and checking our spirit for answers or guidance. He does this by attacking our mind or our body; he cannot attack our spirit. We must continue to take time to get quiet before the Lord so we can hear. We have not been given a spirit of fear. So, if fear is driving you, I can confidently say that you are not being led by the Spirit.

Additionally, verse 21 states we need to prove or test what we are hearing. The first and obvious test is measuring what you hear against the Word of God. The Holy Spirit is never going to prompt us to do something that goes crosswise with the Word. Why is it important to test? Number one, because the Word of God says to, but number two, the enemy will look for opportunities to use confusion or other people to mislead us. We need to test each to see if our spirit has a witness (a peace) about what they are saying. If you don't have peace in your spirit, then you can be confident that what you heard was not from God, and you need to ignore it. We must be sensitive to what God is saying to our spirit so that we can judge our thoughts and what others are saying to us.

So how do we hear our spirit share what the Holy Spirit communicates? One method is highlighted below:

*It seemed good unto us, being assembled with one
accord, to send chosen men unto you with our beloved
Barnabas and Paul.*

Acts 15:25 (KJV)

*For it seemed good to the Holy Ghost, and to us, to lay
upon you no greater burden than these necessary things.*

Acts 15:28 (KJV)

*It seemed good to me also, having had perfect under-
standing of all things from the very first, to write unto
thee in order, most excellent Theophilus, That thou
mightest know the certainty of those things, wherein
thou hast been instructed.*

Luke 1:3–4 (KJV)

These are examples of how believers heard from the Holy
Spirit. They checked inside (checked with their spirit) and sensed
that an action or direction they had considered taking was the
correct one because it *seemed* correct. You could also say they
had a knowing that it was right or good. They didn't reason it
out in their mind. I understand this sounds a bit imprecise and
nebulous, and it certainly can be. We are not always going to
hear as clearly as we would like. However, as with anything else,
the more we practice doing something, the better we will get
at it, and the easier it will be to recognize His voice amongst a
crowd of voices. If we are truly seeking to hear from God, He
will course-correct us if we are heading in a direction where He is
not leading. In John 10:27 (KJV), Jesus said, "My sheep hear my
voice." So we can have confidence in knowing we can.

Let me share how I have found this to work for me. First, I pray for God to provide His wisdom to me as I navigate the challenges of the day. I ask the Holy Spirit to speak to me and provide God's will for me in all situations. Once I have done that, the next step is to stop and check what I am hearing in my spirit. Some days I may make thirty or more decisions. I don't have time to get quiet and pray about each one. I do, however, have time to check my spirit to see if I have a "check" about a decision I am about to make. I provided an example of this in a previous chapter when I talked about the phone conversation I had with a sales representative. When he asked me to share the results of the study, I got a check.

What do I mean when I say I got a check? I had a sense in me that it would not be right, and then the thought reminded me of the commitment I made to the client. The check is in my spirit, not my mind. Some people may refer to this as "conscience." You may have said or heard people say, "My conscience wouldn't let me do that." When believers refer to their consciences, they are most often referring to something they are sensing in their spirit whether they realize it or not.

Back to my example of making decisions, I will consider an issue, arrive at an approach to address the issue, listen for a check, and if I don't get one, make the decision and move on to the next issue. I trust that God will let me know when I am about to make a bad decision. Those that I get a check on (that I don't have peace about), I will shelve until I have time to pray about them to get a clearer direction. I don't always get it right, but over time I have become much better at listening and obeying. It requires a constant focus, which is impossible to do with any consistency if you are not spending regular time with God. How many times have your emotions told you to react to a situation one way, but you've had a knowing from deep inside not to react that way? Perfect example of a check. The more you make it a priority to listen to the Holy Spirit, the better you will be at it. God cares about every decision we make. I told you about the impact my decision not to share the study results with the sales representative had on the organization. I had no idea that decision would affect the way an entire organization viewed me, but God did.

I would like to say I always listen and obey, but I don't. A similar situation occurred when God "checked me" about something I had decided to do, and I did it anyway, resulting in a great big mess. I was working with a client who was paying us to deliver a technical solution. I had delivered similar solutions for several other clients. During the entire development process, two individuals challenged our recommendations for nearly every design decision. After a while, it became clear that neither of them had any real hands-on experience with the technology. They were smart people and had read a lot of articles and books about how to do the work, but they had no practical hands-on experience doing it. We were constantly in conflict over our approach.

Finally, one day I hit my limit. I was physically tired and weary from constantly justifying our approach. I received an email with several questions and few statements about why our proposal was incorrect. It was the last straw. I was hot. I let the emotion die down a bit, yet I still wanted to justify my approach and was crafting a very professional and direct response to the email. I got a check not to do it and ignored it as I typed away. I got another check and ignored it as I pushed the "send" button.

Within a week, we were in a major dispute that took months to resolve. My approach proved to be correct, but because of how I challenged the questions, we ended up doing it the way the individuals suggested, only to find out their approach didn't work, and we had to go back to what we originally proposed. My not acting on the prompting of the Holy Spirit led to months of delay and significant financial impacts on the program. I thought it was more important to justify myself than to listen to what God had to say about the situation. I made it about me and let pride get in the way of listening to God. I am convinced He had a way for me to navigate through the challenge, but I stopped listening by choosing not to act on His leading.

Another way of confirming the Holy Spirit's direction is following peace. The following scriptures talk about following the peace of Christ:

> But the Comforter, which is the Holy Ghost, whom the Father will send in my name, he shall teach you all things, and bring all things to your remembrance, whatsoever I have said unto you. Peace I leave with you, my peace I give unto you: not as the world giveth, give I unto you. Let not your heart be troubled, neither let it be afraid.
>
> John 14:26–27 (KJV)

> And let the peace of God rule in your hearts, to the which also ye are called in one body; and be ye thankful.
>
> Colossians 3:15 (KJV)

Let peace rule your heart and guide your decisions. Often when the Bible refers to the heart, it is not referring to the blood pump in our body. It is referring to our spirit. The scripture is telling us to check our spirit for peace. I cannot stress enough how fundamental this is to defeating Satan's attacks. The next statement is one of the most important points in this entire book. *Following peace does not mean I have an absence of doubt and fear.* I need to say that again: following peace does not mean I have an absence

Following peace does not mean I have an absence of doubt and fear.

of doubt and fear racing through my mind. Fear exists only in our minds. Jesus said He did not give us a *spirit* of fear. It is possible and highly likely that for critical decisions, the enemy has introduced the fear of making a bad decision and has painted a picture in your mind of how terrible it would be to make a particular decision. Yet, when you check your spirit, you find you have peace about the decision.

Your spirit is at peace with the decision while your mind is going crazy with fear and doubt, telling you all sorts of terrible things are going to happen. So, which part of your being are you going to trust? This is so important; we will spend an entire chapter talking about how the devil wants to use fear to stop God's plan for our lives. It was so freeing for me to realize I could have peace in my spirit while still having fear running through my mind. That realization removed a lot of confusion and freed me to make big decisions.

Develop the habit of checking your spirit about every decision and follow peace! This is *huge* and why so many believers struggle. Follow a spirit of peace, and ignore the thoughts of fear and doubt in your mind. You are not waiting for peace in your mind. The enemy can always introduce confusing thoughts into your mind, but He has no access to your spirit. The Bible says what you are hearing in your spirit as a born-again follower of Jesus is coming from the Holy Spirit.

I want to close this chapter by providing something to measure the depth of our walks with the Holy Spirit. Galatians 5:22–24 (AMP) provides that measuring rod:

> But the fruit of the [Holy] Spirit [the work which His presence within accomplishes] is love, joy (gladness), peace, patience (an even temper, forbearance), kindness, goodness (benevolence), faithfulness, Gentleness (meekness, humility), self-control (self-restraint, continence). Against such things there is no law [that can bring a charge]. And those who belong to Christ Jesus (the Messiah) have crucified the flesh (the godless human nature) with its passions and appetites and desires.

As we continue to grow in our walk with God and our relationship with the Holy Spirit, we and those around us should see the fruit of the Spirit manifest in our lives. We should see ourselves become more:

- loving
- joyful (gladness)
- peaceful
- patient (even-tempered, forbearance)
- kind
- good (benevolent)
- faithful
- gentle (meek, humble)
- self-controlled (restrained, continence)

How would you like to work for and with someone who was growing in all of these attributes? If we as believers make it a priority to grow in our relationship with the Holy Spirit, Scripture tells us we will grow in all these areas. If you and I continue to mature each of these attributes, how do you think we will be viewed by those around us? As a leader, what kind of followership do you think we would have?

The Holy Spirit is a tremendous gift provided to us by the Father when we accept Jesus as our Lord and Savior. God speaks His perfect will for us to the Holy Spirit, who, in turn, bears witness to our spirit so we can know God's will in every area of our lives, including our work lives. It is so important for us to realize that and spend time listening to what the Holy Spirit is telling us. This is insight and wisdom that only a follower of Christ can bring into the workplace. It will allow you to deliver unmatched impact wherever God places you. However, it doesn't just fall on you because you are a follower of Christ. You must actively and continually seek to hear from God.

Most importantly, we must not take pride in the results His guidance produces. To continue to hear from God, we must remain humble. God resists the proud, so we must continually resist the pride that can come from our success if we want to continue to hear from God.

I encourage you to set aside quiet time and continue to develop your ability to hear what God is speaking to you by His Word and His Holy Spirit. As we grow in our ability to do this, our impact on our clients, firms, and colleagues goes up exponentially, which is why it is so important we bring our whole self (body, soul, and *spirit*) to our profession.

CHAPTER 8

Walking in Faith and Not Fear

For [the Spirit which] you have now received [is] not a spirit of slavery to put you once more in bondage to fear, but you have received the Spirit of adoption [the Spirit producing sonship] in [the bliss of] which we cry, Abba (Father)! Father!

Romans 8:15 (AMP)

I've discussed in previous chapters how to develop and increase our faith by sowing and hearing the Word, how to hear from the Holy Spirit and expect the Holy Spirit to provide input for all of our decisions, and how to expect that guidance as we operate in our profession. We have touched on only some of the fundamentals. There are many things to learn, and I encourage you to take the scriptures provided in this book as a basis for the beginning or continuation of your study. Commit to learning daily about God's Word and His Holy Spirit.

In this chapter, I want to cover one of the most widely used forces the enemy uses in our lives and the world of business to minimize our success and influence: fear. Our society today is so fear-driven that fear-based actions are viewed as acceptable and even wise. Our news media feeds on exploiting fear, and most of the stories are presented to produce fear, which ultimately drives ratings.

I lived in the DC metro area for over twenty-five years, and whenever there was a chance of snow, it became the top news story for days. You can count on stories where reporters are at the stores, showing empty shelves where bread and milk were once stocked. Inevitably, we will see a reporter at the home improvement store telling us all the snow blowers and snow shovels are sold out. In the event that we got a couple of inches of snow, all schools shut down, and the local news channels took over all the programming for an entire day, telling us how treacherous the roads were and looking for any related problem they could find to showcase.

As someone who grew up in Michigan, I found it humorous that schools were canceled because we got one inch of snow and that people were afraid to go out because the roads may be too dangerous. I'm not suggesting that going out in the middle of a snowstorm is wise, but one to three inches of snow hardly constitutes a snow emergency for someone who grew up in the upper Midwest.

I use this example because the root of it is fear, and fear sells. Tens of thousands, if not hundreds of thousands, in the DC area have been so conditioned by the fear of snow that they will change their daily activities just because of the threat of it.

Fear is prevalent in our society. Whole industries are built upon it. It seems a new phobia is coined each week, and people are spending large portions of their income on techniques to help them manage their fears.

I am not judging those folks, nor am I unsympathetic to their situations. Fear is real and powerful. But it makes me more determined to go after Satan's lies and bring the truth of God's Word to bear for people to use to shut down the author of all fear, Satan. Many of the tactics he uses to steal the sown Word highlighted earlier in the book are based on fear. Jesus said the enemy comes to kill, steal, and destroy. How many times have you seen fear steal joy from someone's life or prevent them from making a decision because they are afraid they will make the wrong one, in effect, stealing their destiny?

The good news is the second half of Jesus' statement says, "but, I have come to give you life and life more abundantly." God has given us His Word and the power of His Holy Spirit to recognize and defeat fear in all its forms. We do not need to be controlled by fear, and if we are, we will never have the joy and impact that God desires.

Fear is the opposite of faith. If you are making decisions based on fear, you are not making them based on faith in God's promises. The flipside of that is if you are making decisions based on faith in the promises of God, you are not making fearful decisions. I have found that fear is always present when I need to make big decisions. The secret is recognizing its presence and responding appropriately when I do. What is an appropriate response? A response based on faith in the promises found in God's Word. Learning how to respond prompted by the Holy Spirit in faith is key to success in all areas of life, particularly as we operate in the world of business.

As a consultant, I have worked at many large organizations and observed the behavior of middle management and leadership as they made what they thought were the safest decisions, those that presented the least risk to them and their careers. Problem is the safest decisions are often not the best long-term decisions for an organization.

I have watched that behavior contribute to a slow decline in organizational performance and ultimately to the failure of the organization. In some cases, the organization's leaders made their decision after weighing the impact it might have on them personally, and the fear of those negative consequences outweighed the possible benefits to their organization and their community. While that sounds like a harsh criticism, it is simply an unfortunate observation.

No one, including Jesus, is immune from fear. The Bible tells us He was tested *No one, including Jesus, is immune from fear.* in all things, so fear had to be one of the things He was tested in. He just never gave in to it. In fact, fear was trying to come against Him in the garden of Gethsemane. He knew what was ahead of Him, and He was agonizing over it. The fear of being separated from God so He could atone for our sins must have been immense. But He overcame it by spending time in prayer with His Father and keeping His eyes on the promise of salvation for all once He completed His suffering. This is the model we too can use to overcome fear in any area of our lives. We can keep our eyes on the promise and stay in contact with God as we walk through to victory, ignoring the fears along the way.

I recognize how easy it is to present this viewpoint and how hard it can be to execute it in our lives. It was hard for Jesus, as well. He was under such pressure in the garden that the Bible said He was sweating blood, yet He stayed focused on the prize and submitted to the will of God and not to fear. Even though I am aware of this truth, at times, I still let the fear drive my decision-making. I am striving to attack fear every time it pops up, however, by using God's Word and the power of His Holy Spirit. In doing so, I become a better leader in my profession and in my family.

As I have observed organizations, God has impressed upon me to assess the motivation behind decisions being made. Many times, I could see a particular decision was based on fear, primarily the fear of losing something. We can be 100 percent confident that if we are making a decision based upon that kind of fear, we are not making the right decision. How can I say that? Because the Word of God says it. Psalm 27:1 (AMP) tells us: "The Lord is my Light and my Salvation—whom shall I fear *or* dread? The Lord is the Refuge *and* Stronghold of my life—of whom shall I be afraid?"

God tells us in John 14:27 (AMP):

> *Peace I leave with you; My [own] peace I now give*
> *and bequeath to you. Not as the world gives do I give*
> *to you. Do not let your hearts be troubled, neither let*
> *them be afraid. [Stop allowing yourselves to be agitated*
> *and disturbed; and do not permit yourselves to be*
> *fearful and intimidated and cowardly and unsettled.]*

God tells us not to be afraid, and He tells us why. Are we going to believe Him, or are we going to join with others and be moved by fear? Will we trust that it is God's will to increase us, or will we trust the fear that says if we do God's will, we may lose something important to us?

As I mentioned, I find fear present every time I need to make a big decision. Over the years, I have made many decisions based on fear. I might have used different wording to camouflage the decision, such as "Because of this concern, or because we need to be careful, I've decided to..." but it was still based on fear

> *Over the years, I have made many decisions in fear. I might have used a different word to camouflage the decision.*

and not on having faith in God's Word and His faithfulness to keep His Word. The point isn't to dwell on the fact that you or I have messed up in the past, but to use those experiences to learn how to recognize the attack and continue to grow in faith so that we succumb to fear less and less. I have learned that I need to remain diligent and test the motivation behind my decisions. If I determine that a particular decision is largely motivated by fear, I know it is a decision I don't need to go through with.

We cannot allow the enemy to use fear to change our focus from meeting the two objectives of business we proposed earlier in the book:

1. To provide goods and services that will allow a community to flourish
2. To serve employees by providing them with opportunities to express at least a portion of their God-given identity through meaningful creative work

To deliver on these two objectives, we must take our focus off ourselves and put it on others. Doing those two things makes it more difficult for the enemy to come at us with fear. Without knowledge of the Word of God and the help of the Holy Spirit, it is impossible to consistently put self in the backseat and ignore fear. After all, isn't selfishness primarily fear-driven? We use a lot of terms to camouflage fear: "I am concerned about this," "I am worried about that," "Let's be careful (or full of care) with this one," "We must protect what we have or what we know."

Each still represents fear. That's what Satan's kingdom operates on. God's kingdom operates on faith. Ironically, Satan is the most fearful being on the planet. As a matter of fact, one of the things he is most afraid of is us walking in the power of faith that God has given His children to walk in and not fear. It is not hard to see that many in the world today are completely controlled by fear. But we as followers of Jesus have been set free from fear. So, let's spend some time analyzing the faith vs. fear dynamic we face daily and how we can use our faith to rise above our fear.

First, when and how did fear enter into the world? Let's look at Genesis 3:9. The fall of man had just taken place. Adam and Eve's eyes were opened, and they went and hid in the garden. Genesis 3:9–10 (KJV) tells us what happened next: "And the Lord God called unto Adam, and said unto him, Where *art* thou? And he said, I heard thy voice in the garden, and I was afraid, because I *was* naked; and I hid myself."

Not only is this the first mention of fear, but this is also an example of how fear *Separation from God will make you fearful.* will affect our judgment, cause us to make bad decisions, and then blame others for the consequences of those decisions. Think about it. The Bible says Adam and Eve had been walking with God for many years, fellowshipping with Him daily. They knew Him, His nature, and His power. Yet after they sinned, they became fearful of God and thought they could hide from Him. Talk about fear clouding your thinking. Where are you going to hide where God can't find you?

Their fear also caused them to decide to separate from God. Think about it. They decided to hide from God and not fellowship with Him. Separation from God will make you fearful. That is why Satan is the most fearful being on the planet: he is completely and eternally separated from God. This is why it is so important for us to set aside time to spend with God in prayer and the study of His Word, no matter what our mind is telling us about our worthiness to spend time with Him. Adam and Eve messed up, and they were afraid to be around God. When we mess up, the enemy will tell us the same thing. His modus operandi has not changed; however, our relationship with God has. If we have accepted Jesus as our Lord and Savior, we need only to humble ourselves, confess our sins, and we are back in right standing with God.

Adam and Eve sinned, God's anointing left them, and fear entered in. Fear is a result of the fall and one of the enemy's favorite tools. He comes at us with:

- The fear of death: God's Word tells me that as a follower of Christ, when I die, I will spend eternity with God. Why should I be afraid of that?
- The fear of failure: God's Word tells me that He blesses all the works of my hands and that it is His will that I prosper. Why would I fear failure?
- The fear of lack: God's Word says He will prosper me in all I do. Why would I fear lack?
- The fear of rejection: God's Word tells me He will never leave me or forsake me, and He will provide favor for me. Why would I fear rejection?

As believers in Christ, we need not be fearful of any of these things. I realize how easy it is to say that and how challenging it is to walk it out. That is why we must meditate on the promises of God. If we have more faith in His promises, we will have less fear of negative consequences.

How does fear manifest itself in the business world? From my experience, it often comes as pressure to get me to do nothing more than compromise my faith in God's promises:

- "I'm not going to make my numbers, and I might lose my job." Instead of believing what God says about the situation, I'll change how I book my numbers or try to take the numbers from someone else.
- "If I don't do this, leadership will think I'm not reliable or a team player, and I won't get the next promotion." Instead of trusting in God's Word that says He will provide His favor and exalt me in His time, do I constantly take time away from my family to demonstrate to others that I am reliable?
- "What will happen if I share the bad news about the project's progress?" Do I trust that God is in control and that being upfront about the status is the right thing to do, or will I just hide it for now because it might get better, and I won't have to let anyone know we are struggling?
- "If I help that person, they might get the promotion I want." Do I believe it's God's will for me to bless those around me, or will I let them figure things out for themselves so I can "fly in" and save the day when the project ends up in a ditch?
- "Do I take responsibility for the current problem?" Do I trust that God is in control and that He has a path through the challenge, or do I place the blame on one of my team members even if it was their fault?

- "Do I take on the new role? I don't think I am ready." Do I believe the Word of God tells me He will make a way for me and that I can do all things through Him, or do I decline the opportunity because I'm afraid I might not be able to do it?

The devil brings pressure from all directions to get our focus off God's promises in the Word so that we will react in fear and make a selfish decision. He is seeking who he can devour. He is trying to kill, steal, and destroy by getting our focus off the promises in the Word by focusing on fear. If we are operating on God's Word backed by the power of the Holy Spirit, the devil knows he has no chance of stopping God's plan for our success, and that scares him like nothing else. When Satan looks at us and sees that we are walking with God, he sees God and knows we will kill, steal, and destroy his plans. He has to convince us that the situation we are facing is too big or too small for God and get us to change our confession of faith. Let's look again at the verse from earlier in our study, Mark 4:19 (AMP): "Then the cares *and* anxieties of the world *and* distractions of the age, and the pleasure *and* delight *and* false glamour *and* deceitfulness of riches, and the craving *and* passionate desire for other things creep in and choke *and* suffocate the Word, and it becomes fruitless."

It is clear from scripture why the fear (cares of this world) come: to choke the Word so it will become unfruitful in our lives. It is a primary mechanism Satan uses to kill, steal, and destroy. He can use fear to steal our joy, for example, by getting us to continually worry about a situation. He can use fear to destroy our relationships when we're always afraid of what someone is saying about us behind our backs.

As long as we live in this world, fear will be ever-present, but we don't have to receive it. We defeat it by standing on God's promises by faith—as the scripture tells us, having done all to stand, stand. We need to develop our faith to take that stand in all areas of our lives. My faith may be highly developed in the area of salvation, for example, but not in the area of finance and giving. Or it may be developed enough to believe that God can heal me of a cold or the flu, but not cancer. I may believe that cancer has a greater ability to kill me than God's ability and desire to heal me.

I do not say these things to bring condemnation but to expand your vision of how God wants to engage in your life and to help build your faith. As we have discussed, we need to recognize that God wants to get involved in all areas of our lives, including our business activities, and He only gets that opportunity when we are standing on His promises in faith.

From my personal observations, fear-based decisions are a primary contributor to the failure of business plans and, ultimately, a business. As a leader, how do you not make decisions primarily based on fear? This, my friend, is an area where we can clearly differentiate a believer from a nonbeliever in the workplace. How do you handle those very real situations where we are being pressured to operate in fear? Whose report will we believe? God's promises or Satan's lies?

One additional thought to ponder here. The Bible says that Satan is the father of all lies and that there is no truth in him. That being the case, if we know Satan is attacking us with fearful thoughts, then we know they are lies. Anything he says is a lie because there is no truth in him. How can we know the thought is from him? First, if it is a thought that does not align with the promises in the Word of God. Second, by the prompting of the

Holy Spirit. I am not talking about denying the circumstances you may find yourself in. I am talking about believing God's promises in the midst of those circumstances. Standing on God's Word and in the power of the Holy Spirit will change those circumstances.

We have the ability to choose what we think about and what we believe. God said in Deuteronomy 30:19 (KJV), "I call heaven and earth to record this day against you, that I have set before you life and death, blessing and cursing: therefore choose life, that both thou and thy seed may live." Matthew 6:30–34 (AMP) tells us which thoughts to choose to keep the cares of this world from controlling us:

> *But if God so clothes the grass of the field, which*
> *today is alive and green and tomorrow is tossed into*
> *the furnace, will He not much more surely clothe you,*
> *O you of little faith? Therefore do not worry and be*
> *anxious, saying, What are we going to have to eat?*
> *or, What are we going to have to drink? or, What are*
> *we going to have to wear? For the Gentiles (heathen)*
> *wish for and crave and diligently seek all these things,*
> *and your heavenly Father knows well that you need*
> *them all. But seek (aim at and strive after) first of*
> *all His kingdom and His righteousness (His way of*
> *doing and being right), and then all these things taken*
> *together will be given you besides. So do not worry or*
> *be anxious about tomorrow, for tomorrow will have*
> *worries and anxieties of its own. Sufficient for each day*
> *is its own trouble.*

To combat the fear, we need to do the same thing that Jesus did when He was confronted by the devil, and that is speak the Word to him and the situation. We need to develop our faith to the point where we see those previous verses as reality. When we have more faith in God's ability and desire to clothe us and be our source than we do in our ability to play that role, then we don't have to be afraid of losing our jobs. It frees me up to make the bold decision when required. I know my job is not my source. It is just one of the channels that God (my source) is using to bless me.

As someone who is a Driver or Type A personality, I find it very challenging not to trust in my ability to make things happen. Based on experience and reading the Word, I intellectually understand how limited my ability is to change something significantly. Yet, I find when things get tough, I think I can just work harder, and that will take care of the problem. When the fear or pressure really comes upon me, it is a signal that I need to get quiet before God and not just work harder. I need to hear His answer to the challenge and not just rely on my hard work or the hard work of others to overcome the challenge.

Over time, I have become better at not just trying to work harder but to allow God to get involved. It is hard for God to get involved if I am trying to do everything. It means I am not giving Him an opportunity, and He never forces His way in. Instead, I am working too hard and not setting aside time to listen to Him. Fear will make you think you need to work harder to fix the problem. It will try to speed you up and take away the quiet time you spend with God.

Over the years, in these situations, I have learned it is crucial to spend time with God first to understand what my part is and let God handle His part. When I hear the thought that I don't have time to spend with God because I must get something done, I know it is a lie and fear-based. The Word of God says, "Seek ye first the kingdom of God…"

Don't get me wrong; you will have to work hard. But if I am taking time to hear from God, the hard work will produce a good end. I would rather see that than work hard and still fail. It takes time and effort on our part to develop our faith to that level, but it is time well spent, and once we get to that point, we need to remain consistent in spending time with Him so we can remain in that place.

Even though I know this, I can find myself caught up in working extra hard to address a situation and not taking the time to ask for help and guidance from God. Thankfully, in those instances, when I get tired enough, I finally recognize what is going on and ask for His help. God is always merciful and willing to engage with me. I just need to ask in faith. Remember, we develop our faith by hearing the Word: "Faith comes by hearing and hearing the Word of God." How do we know how great (or how little) our faith is? The scriptures below provide a way to measure our faith:

> *"O generation of vipers, how can ye, being evil, speak good things? for out of the abundance of the heart the mouth speaketh."*
>
> Matthew 12:34 (KJV)

> *The upright (honorable, intrinsically good) man out of the good treasure [stored] in his heart produces what is upright (honorable and intrinsically good), and the evil man out of the evil storehouse brings forth that*

which is depraved (wicked and intrinsically evil); for
out of the abundance (overflow) of the heart his mouth
speaks.

Luke 6:45 (AMP)

When the pressure comes and the fear associated with it shows up, what do you say? Do you hear fear-filled words or faith-filled words coming out of you? Be sensitive to the words you say. If you notice that your words are filled with care or fear, that is the signal to spend more time hearing the Word of God and to dwell on His promises and not just the issue at hand. If you are making decisions based upon fear, you are making bad decisions.

I'm not saying that to offend. I am saying that because that is what the Word of God says, and I have witnessed this many times over my career. We must choose what we believe, as the Word says, and the confession will happen naturally based on what is in your heart and spirit. Deuteronomy 30:19 (AMP) tells us that God gives us that freedom, and He rewards those who choose His way of life: "I call heaven and earth to witness this day against you that I have set before you life and death, the blessings and the curses; therefore choose life, that you and your descendants may live."

Followers of Christ can make choices based on fear. We all make them. We let the cares of the world enter at times, choke our faith, and prevent us from walking in all that God has provided through His Word and His Holy Spirit. So, what do you do when you realize you have made a bad choice? You humble yourself, ask for forgiveness, believe that you have received it by faith, go forward, and trust that God will help you recover from it. God is a loving God and a God of grace. He knows we are imperfect, we don't know everything, and our faith is not developed in every area. He looks at our heart. Thank God He has given us His Holy Spirit (as a helper, advocate, etc.) to help us navigate the challenges we face daily and to help us grow in understanding. So, go forward and speak words of life, God's Word, over life's challenges.

Our ability to walk in faith and not fear distinguishes us from nonbelievers in the workplace. The way we react to pressure and fear is very noticeable. We have the ability to walk in confidence, not to be confused with arrogance, through the most challenging situations in the workplace. We are not confident in ourselves but in God's promises and His desire to see them come to pass to impact the lives of those around us.

Do we treat people differently when we are under pressure and fearful? Do we levy blame and deflect responsibility? Or do we look to help those who are struggling through a situation? In high-pressure situations, do we attack people for not doing their jobs? Or do we take the bad news and work with them to find a solution? People around us notice. Some people have pointed out in my 360-degree reviews that "Derick is one of the few people who can take you to the woodshed, but you feel good about yourself when he is done."

I don't share that to exalt myself. I share that because it is a measure of God's presence in me. God is love, and He wants us to show that love toward those we interact with in all situations. It just becomes more evident in the high-pressure situations where fear is ever-present. It does not mean we don't hold people accountable for what their role is. It means we deal with them differently than others may when they don't meet expectations.

We don't respond in fear, we don't attack, and we don't condemn. We respond with grace and God's love when we correct them.

This leads me to discuss another fear, the fear of people not liking us. Often people are afraid to confront others because of the results it may produce. Part of the reason for that are the examples of confrontation we see in the workplace are not done in love. They are often driven by frustration, anger, selfishness, or self-preservation. The results are often hurt, distrust, and discord. Confrontation is required at times, but it can be done in love and not anger or selfishness. When done properly, it does not create discord; it encourages and builds up. We can't let the fear of upsetting someone prevent us from providing the required feedback to address an issue to help that individual be successful.

I previously shared an example of a time when I didn't do this in love. A couple of people in influential positions were continually challenging my approach to a situation, and I let pride creep in because I felt they did not have the practical experience I possessed. I finally confronted them, not in love but to exalt me. I was acting in fear, fear that my opinion was not being respected as I felt it should have been. I did it professionally, but, bottom line, I was not acting in faith. I was acting out of fear of not being respected as the expert.

That situation resulted in both the client and me losing. I lost my influence with them, and they went forth with the approach they had defined. They lost because their approach failed, and it cost them a few million dollars. Then they had to implement what I had suggested in the first place. I was tired, did not listen to the promptings of the Holy Spirit, and acted in fear. I wish I hadn't gone through the pain of learning that lesson, but it was a valuable one.

To summarize, from my experience, how you handle pressure and fear is the most important factor in determining success in the business world. It is always going to come, and as you progress in your career, it can be more intense, and your actions have the potential to impact more people positively or negatively. Will you believe God's report, use your faith, and stand strong? Remember, faith comes by hearing and hearing by the Word of God.

Finally, remember that even when you mess up (and you will; we all do), you can and should humble yourself, repent, and ask forgiveness. Often for me, believing that God forgives me as soon as I ask Him for it requires the most faith. Thank God for His grace. John 14:27 (KJV) promises that God's peace is for us: "Peace I leave with you, my peace I give unto you: not as the world giveth, give I unto you. Let not your heart be troubled, neither let it be afraid."

How powerful it is when we operate this way in the business world. What a difference we bring for others to see. Trust that it is God's desire to bless you in all things, and know that we don't need to operate in fear because it is not from God. God will give you the platform and His wisdom to boldly lead. People will gravitate to that type of calm, consistent leadership.

CHAPTER 9

Operating and Leading in Righteousness

Cast your burden on the Lord [releasing the weight of it] and He will sustain you; He will never allow the [consistently] righteous to be moved (made to slip, fall, or fail).

Psalm 55:22 (AMP)

All that we have studied up to this point builds the foundation for what we are going to discuss in this chapter. How do we use what God has provided through His grace, His Word, and His Holy Spirit to impact those within our sphere of influence in a positive way? It may be obvious to some, but I need to be 100 percent clear by what I mean when I say, "operating in righteousness." I will start by saying what it does not mean. It does not mean that we are self-righteous, that we judge others by their actions and have an inflated view of ourselves based on how effective we think we are at keeping a set of rules or doing good deeds.

We spent an entire chapter talking about God's grace. That is His gift to us, and once we received it, we received right standing (righteousness) with God. You may ask, "Why does that matter in my vocation?" It is a fair question and one we will consider in the next few pages. Let's start by looking at what it means to operate in righteousness.

First, it is important not to confuse righteousness with holiness. You may find the terms used interchangeably, but they are very different. Holiness means being set aside, consecrated, and sanctified for the service of the Lord. Righteousness is right standing with God. It is about what He has done for us through grace. Both are important, but they are two completely different concepts.

We want to discuss what it means to be able to stand before God, knowing we are in right standing with Him. Let's look into the scriptures and see what it means to be righteous. In these pages, I can only touch on the significance of our right standing with God. I encourage you to comb through your Bible and find those passages that describe the blessings God pours out on the righteous; there are hundreds. A great place to start is the book of Proverbs. It is packed with promises made to the righteous. However, let's start by looking at what Psalm 112:2–9 (AMP) says about the righteous.

> *His [spiritual] offspring shall be mighty upon earth; the generation of the upright shall be blessed. Prosperity and welfare are in his house, and his righteousness endures forever. Light arises in the darkness for the upright, gracious, compassionate, and just [who are in right standing with God]. It is well with the man who deals generously and lends, who conducts his affairs with justice. He will not be moved forever; the [uncompromisingly] righteous (the upright, in right standing with God) shall be in everlasting remembrance. He shall not be afraid of evil tidings; his heart is firmly fixed, trusting (leaning on and being confident) in the Lord. His heart is established and steady, he will not be*

afraid while he waits to see his desire established upon
his adversaries. He has distributed freely [he has given
to the poor and needy]; his righteousness (uprightness
and right standing with God) endures forever; his horn
shall be exalted in honor.

These verses provide a description of the type of employee or leader we can expect to become as followers of Christ:

1. We will be mighty on the earth: we will have influence, and we will be able to impact many for good.
2. We will be prosperous: we help our employer prosper, and we will prosper, not just financially, but in every area of our lives as a result of wise decisions and walking in love.
3. We will bring illumination: light will arise out of darkness. We will have insight to provide solutions to problems and challenges that others cannot because we have the light of God in us.
4. It will be well with us because we conduct our affairs with justice; we are not just looking to enrich ourselves.
5. We will be stable: we will not be moved by the changing values in the society around us or the problems of the day. We will be consistent because our hearts are firmly fixed on God.
6. We will not be moved by fear: we are firmly fixed on the promises of God and know that He blesses the righteous.

7. We are givers: we are willing to share our financial resources with the poor and be a blessing to those in our sphere of influence by sharing our time, expertise, and wisdom.

This is a pretty impressive list of blessings that God promises to the people in right standing with Him. How much of this will you receive and believe? What measure will you mete? Can you see yourself operating daily in these blessings? If so, how would that change the influence you have in your profession, your family, and your community? Do those who interact with you daily view you as stable, unafraid of the challenges of the day, and generous? If not, the Word says you can be, and in God's eyes, you already are.

I don't make this point to condemn anyone. I make it to answer the question of what righteousness has to do with how we operate daily in our profession. By grace, we have the righteousness of Christ. As the righteous of God, we have access to each of these blessings, which God freely gives. We need to do nothing to earn them. However, we do need to receive them, and we must receive them by faith.

We've already discussed how to do that. First, we need to sow these promises from the Word of God and continually confess them. Second, we need to increase

> *These promises are made to every believer; we determine how real they become in our lives.*

our vision and faith in these areas. We previously discussed how to do that, as well. Faith comes by hearing and hearing by the Word of God. We need to fill our ears and hearts with the Word. Our confession is part of that. We hear the Word when we speak it. We must devote time to studying and hearing the Word of God. To walk in the blessings noted above, we need to commit to spending time with God. By faith, we must see ourselves excelling in each of these areas. God makes these promises to every believer. We determine how real they become in our lives. Let's look at a few more of the promises God made to the righteous. Second Corinthians 9:10 (AMP) tells us that God will increase the fruits of our righteousness: "And [God] Who provides seed for the sower and bread for eating will also provide and multiply your [resources for] sowing and increase the fruits of your righteousness [which manifests itself in active goodness, kindness, and charity]."

God blesses the works of our hands and increases the fruits of our righteousness, which manifest themselves in active goodness, kindness, and charity. God provides the seeds; we must continually get better at being focused on the needs of those around us. The easy one to see is the increase in financial resources we can contribute to the poor, but He also provides seeds in more subtle ways. He provides us with experience and expertise that we can sow into those around us in our professional environments.

How many times have you seen examples of individuals holding onto information and not sharing it with their peers because they thought it gave them job security? God is telling us to do just the opposite. He is telling us to share that information and to trust Him to provide us more "seeds" of wisdom and knowledge, not to keep but to sow into those around us. It is a process that continues to expand. We sow into others to help them grow, our influence increases, and God increases the seeds (wisdom, knowledge, and experience) so we can share them. It is hard to slip into greed and selfishness if we take this perspective with the blessings God provides the righteous.

While this would be enough, God has promised us even more. Let's look at Proverbs 13:22 (AMP): "A good man leaves an inheritance [of moral stability and goodness] to his children's children, and the wealth of the sinner [finds its way eventually] into the hands of the righteous, for whom it was laid up."

As I have matured as a believer, I have come to see a bigger vision related to this verse. I started by personalizing it by believing that God was taking the wealth of the wicked and transferring it to me. There is truth to that, but there was also a lot of me in that viewpoint, which made my thinking very narrow because it was focused solely on me. I now have a bigger (and a more mature) vision of what that verse means for the righteous in business.

It is not just about the wealth that God provides me as an individual. It is more about the resources He puts me in charge of in my role within an organization. For example, we could find ourselves in a role that gives us profit and loss (P&L) responsibility for an organization with annual revenue of $150,000,000. In that role, we would have the responsibility of managing a large budget and making decisions about where and how investments are made in our employees, products, clients, and communities.

We would be responsible for making investments that help our employees grow, develop, and deliver products and services that help a community flourish. This is not a hypothetical situation. It is one that I found myself in, so I understand what that level of influence means and why it is important to the kingdom of God. What kind of impact could a group of believers in a community have if they had the responsibility of leading many of the largest businesses in that community?

I worked in the Washington, DC, metro area for years. What would happen if a group of God's people walking in His righteousness was responsible for managing large government-run social programs? Could they meet the needs of the people better than unbelievers, using the same funds? Yes. I don't say that out of pride or because I believe Christians are better than everyone else, and I don't say that to offend anyone. I say that because the Bible tells us it is so. In Proverbs 11:10 (AMP) and Proverbs 29:2 (AMP), we see that people rejoice when the righteous are in power and do well: "When it goes well with the [uncompromisingly] righteous, the city rejoices, but when the wicked perish, there are shouts of joy"; "When the [uncompromisingly] righteous are in authority, the people rejoice; but when the wicked man rules, the people groan *and* sigh."

One of the desires of my heart and a key driver for me writing this book is to help believers see themselves in these types of roles and help them develop their knowledge of God's Word and will so we can have a positive impact on millions of people. What kind of impact on the human condition would we see if believers were walking in the truths we have discussed and leading programs that disbursed tens or hundreds of billions of dollars annually to the poor? Would there be less abuse of funds and less partisanship? Would there be less confusion and strife swirling around the programs? I firmly believe the answer is yes, and I believe it is God's desire for His people to be in those positions to impact communities for the better.

But we cannot get there just by going to church once a week. The enemy is not going to turn over the riches of this world without a fight. As a matter of fact, he will never turn them over. We need to take them, and we do that by landing in positions of influence. We need to spend time in the Word and know what God's promises say so we can develop a big vision and stand in faith for the results of those promises.

The definition of a big vision is different for everyone. To understand what it is for each of us, we need to spend time in prayer and in the Word to develop a relationship with the Holy Spirit so we can follow His leading. God has a great plan for all of us, and only He can lead us into it. Psalm 5:12 (AMP) tells us it is God's will to bless and protect the righteous: "For You, Lord, will bless the [uncompromisingly] righteous [him who is upright and in right standing with You]; as with a shield You will surround him with goodwill (pleasure and favor)."

This is something I pray before I enter a big meeting or an important interaction with a client or potential client and why it is important for me to recognize that I have right standing with God. I trust that His favor is upon me, not because of anything I have done, but because by grace, I am one of His righteous. It is God's desire for His favor to be on you as you deal with clients, customers, employees, and co-workers.

This has been the big differentiator in my career. I humbly expect God's favor to be upon me as I interact daily in business, not because I am special or because I have performed a good work or earned it in some way. It is solely because I have received the gift of His righteousness through grace. Because of that, I am positioned for Him to bless all that I do that is aligned with His will.

Will you believe that God's favor is on you in your business dealings independent of how polished you are, who you know, or where you went to school? None of that matters to God. He already knows all those things about you and has placed you in that role anyway. Even if any of those earthly qualifications matter to those you interact with, God's favor will open all the doors you need. I say that from experience.

God's favor and the leading of the Holy Spirit will position you and differentiate you from others. When that happens, we must remember it's not about us. It is about the influence it provides us to impact others. Once you get that promotion or position of influence, you can easily fall into pride. We must resist that because God resists the proud, and we need His help to deliver the impact He desires.

There have been multiple times in my career where my client, my leadership, or the members of my teams have come to me and mentioned there is something different about me and how I lead. Some feel a level of comfort in sharing concerns. Some trust me because they believe I am looking out for their best interests, not just my own. Or I may say or do the specific thing someone needs in the moment. I don't often know what people need to hear or how they need to hear it, but God does, and that is where His favor comes in. He helps me with what to say and when to say it by speaking to me via the Holy Spirit. Many times, I have been in a meeting and said something I had not planned and realized afterward that it was just the right thing. This is just one example of how God's favor comes. As you press into the biblical truths presented in this book, you will experience it, as well. Once you have experienced the reality of God's favor, it will create a hunger to experience it again and again. Trust Him and not your own understanding.

Self-promotion has become such an accepted practice in our society today that we're often viewed as lacking something if we do not engage in it. Leaders I respect have told me on multiple occasions that I needed to promote myself more. I need to be more excited about the things I have done and to make leadership aware of them. They provided that advice out of respect and concern for me, and I really appreciated their willingness to do so. Yet, the Scripture teaches me something different. It tells me about the trouble and ruin a prideful man will fall into, but most importantly, it also tells me that God will promote me, that His favor will be upon me. In Job 36:7 (AMP), God tells us He will exalt the righteous: "He withdraws not His eyes from the righteous (the upright in right standing with God); but He sets them forever with kings upon the throne, and they are exalted."

God will exalt us; we don't need to do it. We must trust and believe that He will. This is a hard truth to stand on in the business world because so many people are promoting and exalting themselves. This is not a criticism. After all, if someone does not know God, what else do they have to base their understanding on? They can only rely on what they see modeled in the organization in which they work.

How many of God's people are demonstrating a different approach? Because "getting ahead" is so prevalent in the western culture today, you can expect the cares of this world to continually creep in and tell you that if you don't promote yourself, you are falling behind, and you won't get that promotion. Don't believe it! God's Word says otherwise. It is the enemy coming to steal the Word from you and kill your crop.

Many years ago, I was working at a firm and started to develop some thinking and market offerings around the use of data in the enterprise. The need was being driven by a client, and I was working with my team to develop solutions for that client. At the same time, God was showing me the need was bigger than just one client, so I started to share that within my firm. Over the next few months, my team and I were able to develop an impressive set of solutions just as the market started to seek them. At that time, God created two connections for me that ultimately expanded my influence beyond what I could have imagined a few weeks earlier.

The first was a request from a team that was developing a very large opportunity centered on the topic my team had spent the previous eight months developing. The team asked me to help them pursue the opportunity, and I agreed. After engaging, I found out it was a $100,000,000 deal! In the mid to late nineties, that was an enormous deal, much bigger than anything I had supported to that point in time.

In a few days, I found myself with executives at the client site meeting to discuss my firm's capabilities. I spent time in preparation with the team, understanding the client's challenges and preparing the key points we wanted to make during the discussion. I also spent time alone praying in the Spirit and asking for God's favor to be on me in the discussion.

Our plan was to have the account team drive most of the discussion. I was to provide input around my area of expertise when the account team called on me. Shortly after introductions, I found myself front and center at the whiteboard for 75 percent of the meeting, fielding questions and walking the client through business and technical scenarios that each executive wanted to discuss. This went on for about forty-five minutes. This was not exactly how we planned for the meeting to go, but God was exalting me.

Within a week, we were awarded the contract. God's favor was on me. I didn't try to position myself as the guy to drive the discussion. God opened the door, and I was prepared for the opportunity. When God opens the door, we must be prepared. God did His part by providing the opportunity, and I did my part by being prepared. I don't know for sure, but that opportunity may have never come if I hadn't been skilled in my craft.

Without that preparation, I would have had nothing of value to share with the prospective clients.

Within a couple of weeks of that experience, I was scheduled to present the solutions my team had been developing to one of my firm's senior vice presidents. This individual ran a business unit with revenues greater than one billion dollars a year. The meeting was scheduled for thirty minutes and ended up running for two hours. Anytime you can keep a senior executive's attention focused for thirty minutes, you have done something. God's favor was upon me.

Later that week, I was sitting with co-workers at a table in the cafeteria when the senior vice president came by and said in front of everyone, "The presentation you made the other day was one of the best presentations I have seen." Wow, God's favor was on it, and God was exalting me.

A few weeks later, my wife and I were invited to a dinner celebrating the $100,000,000 win. It was at a restaurant and began with hors d'oeuvres, drinks, and people milling around and talking. All of the business unit's top executives were in attendance, and I could see some of the folks positioning to converse with senior leaders. When it was time for dinner, we had to pick a table. Each table could only seat six people, or three couples. If you've ever been in a situation like this, you've probably seen the way folks will try to position themselves to sit with the most senior leaders. This event was no different.

My wife and I picked a table in the back and sat down. Much to our surprise, the senior vice president and her husband came back and sat at our table. This was God's favor at work. Later during our dinner, the vice president said to my wife that I was a rising star in the organization. God was exalting me in His time. I had spent nearly a year developing solutions to meet a client's need, and God used that to exalt me to a new level of influence. Experiences like that will build your faith and trust in the Lord. Remember, He is no respecter of persons. He will do it for all who believe.

We are God's people, His righteous, and He has committed to us that He will watch out for us. The following scriptures confirm that commitment:

- Psalm 34:15 (AMP): "The eyes of the Lord are toward the [uncompromisingly] righteous and His ears are open to their cry."
- First Peter 3:12 (AMP): "For the eyes of the Lord are upon the righteous (those who are upright and in right standing with God), and His ears are attentive to their prayer. But the face of the Lord is against those who practice evil [to oppose them, to frustrate, and defeat them]."
- Proverbs 10:3 (AMP): "The Lord will not allow the [uncompromisingly] righteous to famish, but He thwarts the desire of the wicked."
- Psalm 34:17 (AMP): "When the *righteous* cry for help, the Lord hears, and delivers them out of all their distress *and* troubles."
- Proverbs 15:29 (AMP): "The Lord is far from the wicked, but He hears the prayer of the [consistently] righteous (the upright, in right standing with Him)."
- Proverbs 10:24 (AMP): "The thing a wicked man fears shall come upon him, but the desire of the [uncompromisingly] righteous shall be granted."

- Psalm 55:22 (AMP): "Cast your burden on the Lord [releasing the weight of it] and He will sustain you; He will never allow the [consistently] righteous to be moved (made to slip, fall, or fail)."
- Proverbs 11:28 (AMP): "He who leans on, trusts in, *and* is confident in his riches shall fall, but the [uncompromisingly] righteous shall flourish like a green bough."
- Isaiah 32:17 (AMP): "And the effect of righteousness will be peace [internal and external], and the result of righteousness will be quietness and confident trust forever."
- Proverbs 15:6 (AMP): "In the house of the [uncompromisingly] righteous is great [priceless] treasure, but with the income of the wicked is trouble *and* vexation."
- Proverbs 3:32 (AMP): "For the perverse are an abomination [extremely disgusting and detestable] to the Lord; but His confidential communion *and* secret counsel are with the [uncompromisingly] righteous (those who are upright and in right standing with Him)."

Why is our right standing with God important? Because God's promises are to the righteous. The last scripture says His confidential communion and secret counsel are with the righteous. How powerful is that? What an advantage we have. His attention, favor, protection, and blessings are on the righteous. We need to meditate on the fact that by grace, we are the righteous and the recipients of all the blessings that come with it.

Having a solid understanding of the blessings of the righteous will cause us to operate in our vocation in a manner that distinguishes us from others. We can resist fear, we can be stable, and we can be givers of knowledge and finances. Most importantly, we can rest in knowing that God's favor will be on us as we walk in His will and that He will exalt us in His time. It is His desire for us to increase in resources and influence and use that increase to bless those around us and spread the gospel to expand His kingdom.

CHAPTER 10

Operating and Leading in Wisdom

The beginning of Wisdom is: get Wisdom (skillful and godly Wisdom)! [For skillful and godly Wisdom is the principal thing.] And with all you have gotten, get understanding (discernment, comprehension, and interpretation).

Proverbs 4:7 (AMP)

We spent the previous chapter talking about why it is important to operate in righteousness so we can deliver a greater impact in our careers. In this chapter, we are going to talk about operating confidently in the wisdom of God daily and the impact it brings. Let's start by looking at the relationship between wisdom and righteousness. Proverbs 10:31 (AMP) provides the insight: "The mouths of the righteous (those harmonious with God) bring forth skillful and godly Wisdom, but the perverse tongue shall be cut down [like a barren and rotten tree]."

This scripture tells us that God provides His wisdom to the righteous, who, in turn, speak it. We know we are God's righteous, so godly wisdom is available to us. In the Amplified Bible, wisdom is often referred to as skillful and godly wisdom. As a matter of fact, Proverbs, written by Solomon, who is often referred to as the wisest man who ever lived, contains that phrase at least twenty-five times. It is obviously important, so we would do well to understand what God is saying through Solomon about wisdom. So, let's start by unpacking what skillful and godly wisdom is. Below is the definition of each:

- *Skillful*: having the training, knowledge, and experience needed to do something well
- *Godly*: conforming to the laws and wishes of God
- *Wisdom*: knowledge and the capacity to make use of it; knowledge of the best ends and the best means; discernment and judgment; discretion

If we put it all together, we find that skillful and godly wisdom is having the training, knowledge, and experience needed to do something well while conforming to the laws and wishes of God and demonstrating the capacity to make use of knowledge through discernment, judgment, and discretion to identify the best means to achieve the best ends.

What a mouthful. Yet how insightful and powerful.

The expanded definition provides several points to discuss. First, as we discussed previously, the responsibility for being skillful lies primarily with us. We must take the time and have the discipline to obtain the training and knowledge and then work to obtain the experience to understand how to do something well. That is our responsibility; it will not fall out of the sky. We can't sit in front of the TV or surf the web for three to five hours a day and expect to be skillful at anything except how to surf the web and watch TV.

I don't say this to condemn; I say this to make a point. It takes work, dedication, and discipline to become skillful at anything. Olympic athletes do not make it to that level of competition without spending thousands of hours developing their God-given athletic skills through hard work and a disciplined lifestyle. Similarly, to run the race and obtain the prize God has promised, we will need to work and develop our skills and knowledge in whatever vocation God has placed us.

Second, we must study the Word of God so we know how to conform our work to the laws and wishes of God. We have mentioned often in the preceding chapters how we may approach aligning the work we do to God's laws and wishes:

1. Provide goods and services that will allow a community to flourish
2. Serve employees by providing them with opportunities to express at least a portion of their God-given identity through meaningful, creative work

While these two objectives are very broad, as we study the Word of God and understand more about His nature and how to conform our thinking and actions to His desires, we will find ourselves making small decisions that are moving what we do in His direction. Just as it is with developing our skills, learning how to conform our skills to God's laws and wishes takes time, effort, and discipline on our part. We must spend time in God's Word and in prayer if we have any hope of getting there.

It is important to realize we must balance the development of our skills and the godly nature He desires. It is folly to think we can spend all our time developing our skills to get to a point of influence and think we are now in a position to make decisions that will bless God and positively impact the community and our colleagues. If we are not knowledgeable of God's ways before we get to that point, it is highly unlikely that we will be prepared to operate in a godly fashion once the pressure of that position begins to build.

Conversely, we can't spend all our time studying the Word of God and expect to be skillful in our profession unless we are in full-time paid ministry positions. The skills and experience required will not just happen because we believe in God. We must put forth the effort to become skillful in our craft.

Finally, demonstrating the capacity to make use of knowledge through discernment, judgment, and discretion to identify the best means to achieve the best ends comes from trusting the Holy Spirit to provide the guidance and understanding to pull it all together in an impactful manner. God has committed to doing His part of the equation.

He provides us the ability to understand how to use the knowledge and skill we possess to identify the best means to achieve the best ends. How does He do that? Through guidance provided by His Word and His Holy Spirit. God will give us wisdom for everything we do if we ask Him and listen for His answer. We must spend time in prayer making our requests known to God and then listening to the prompting of the Holy Spirit that provides the discernment, judgment, and discretion required to make wise decisions. As we discussed previously, we will get a check in our spirit if we are about to head in the wrong direction, but we will find peace in our spirit about a correct decision. The equation for success and impact is simple:

((Natural knowledge + skill) + knowledge of God's principles) x God's wisdom = big impact.

Following this simple equation allows followers of Jesus to deliver impact in whatever their profession far beyond those who don't access the wisdom of God.

Let me provide a simple example of the role God's wisdom plays in delivering impact. I am an amateur woodworker. When I get ready to make a piece of furniture, I will pull together the plan, the raw materials, and any additional tools needed to produce the piece. However, I inevitably need more. I have a certain skill level obtained from past projects, but the new project may require jointing or staining techniques, neither of which I have experience with. So, what do I do? I go to a source that can provide insight on the techniques. I search YouTube for videos that demonstrate how to do what is lacking in my skill and knowledge.

Just as the YouTube video closes the understanding gap for me, God's wisdom provides the additional understanding required to show me how to apply the resources, experience, and skills I have available to address the challenge I am faced with. In both cases, something very important is required: humility. Humility is recognizing that I don't know everything I need to know, and I need to seek a source that can provide the insight required for me to close the gap.

God's wisdom not only closes that gap but it provides the vision to deliver exceptional results. It doesn't just allow us to deliver a result; it allows us to deliver the best result. Walking in God's wisdom will differentiate believers from nonbelievers because God's wisdom is always right! We have access to it because He freely gives it.

Will we make it a priority to spend the time to obtain it? It is invaluable to those who are trying to solve business or social problems. You can have twelve PhDs after your name, but you cannot educate yourself enough to understand all the permutations associated with a decision, and you will never know what will happen in the future and how to factor that into your decision. But God knows the future, He knows the answer to every problem, and He wants to share it with His people (you and me), so we can bless others and expand His kingdom.

Are you calling on Him? Do you think He doesn't care because it is business-related? We have learned that is not true. He will provide answers to every question. Are you asking, and are you listening?

Wisdom shows us how to take the knowledge and talents we possess to impact the world around us. That statement is so important. Spend time thinking about that and how you have seen it played out in situations in your life. I would argue that without wisdom, knowledge is of little value.

When does knowledge have value? The world says it has value when you can apply the knowledge you have to address a problem or meet a need. The bigger the problem you can solve, the more the world values your contribution, and the more influence and compensation the world system provides. Success in these areas is not based on how much knowledge you have but on how effectively you use the knowledge you have.

How often have you encountered someone who is highly educated but who makes destructive, head-scratching decisions or they can't make a decision at all? That is an example of someone who has knowledge but lacks the wisdom to know how to leverage that knowledge to positively impact those around them.

In the world, wisdom is often confused with intelligence. I did not go to a top university nor graduate with academic honors, but others over the years have viewed me as very intelligent. But it was not my intelligence. It was the wisdom of God showing me how to apply the knowledge I or others had to meet a need. I ask God for it every day and try to apply it in every situation. Do I always get it right? No, but am I better at it now than I was ten years ago? Yes, and I desire to be better at it five years from now. This requires humility.

Once you realize wisdom is the key to success, you must also know it is not your skill or intelligence that produces the successful results. If this is your perspective, then it is impossible to be full of pride because you understand how much of your success is dependent on the gifts of God.

Over the years, I have been in so many meetings where there was turmoil, and I was able to speak into the situation what I believed I heard from the Lord, and the entire discussion changed. Now when I say I heard from the Lord, I don't mean I heard an audible voice or that I received some revelation that knocked me to the floor. It is a thought that came to me that I checked against my spirit to see if I had peace or a knowing about. I don't do this all the time. Sometimes the emotion of the meeting can get in the way, and I don't take time to check my spirit, but the opportunity to do so is still available. This is an example of drawing on God's wisdom. Because I am righteous, I can come boldly to God's throne and ask for help in my time of need.

Wisdom is an area that can clearly distinguish believers from unbelievers in the marketplace. It comes from having right standing with God, by His grace, and believing by faith that He will provide His wisdom when we seek it. We obtain wisdom from God's Word and the promptings of His Holy Spirit. Let's see what Proverbs 2:6–12 (AMP) has to say about wisdom.

For the Lord gives skillful and godly Wisdom; from
His mouth come knowledge and understanding. He
hides away sound and godly Wisdom and stores it
for the righteous (those who are upright and in right
standing with Him); He is a shield to those who walk
uprightly and in integrity, That He may guard the
paths of justice; yes, He preserves the way of His saints.
Then you will understand righteousness, justice, and
fair dealing [in every area and relation]; yes, you will
understand every good path. For skillful and godly
Wisdom shall enter into your heart, and knowledge
shall be pleasant to you. Discretion shall watch over
you, understanding shall keep you, To deliver you from
the way of evil and the evil men, from men who speak
perverse things and are liars.

How powerful is that? God tells us we will understand every good path. How important is that to someone trying to solve a business or social problem? I'll tell you, it is the recipe for success. Who does God say it is available to? God's righteous, you and me. This verse also says wisdom will enter our hearts or, as we have discussed, our spirit. What a promise. God said He would give us wisdom; how do we obtain it? Proverbs 9:10–11 (AMP) tells us: "The reverent *and* worshipful fear of the Lord is the beginning (the chief and choice part) of Wisdom, and the knowledge of the Holy One is insight *and* understanding. For by me [Wisdom from God] your days shall be multiplied, and the years of your life shall be increased."

Verse 10 tells us that reverent and worshipful fear of the Lord is the beginning of wisdom. That does not mean we should be afraid of the Lord. It means that an understanding of who

God is, a respect for and an attitude of worshiping God, and the knowledge that He is the source of wisdom, is the beginning of wisdom. It is a recognition that God is more intelligent than we are and being thankful that He will share His understanding with us.

If we don't believe God is the Alpha and the Omega, the beginning and the end, the Creator and Orchestrator of the universe, then why would we even ask His opinion on anything? However, if we recognize God for who He is, humble ourselves, and diligently seek Him and His wisdom, Scripture promises we will be blessed. God tells us how important wisdom is in Proverbs 8:11–12 (AMP): "For skillful and godly Wisdom is better than rubies or pearls, and all the things that may be desired are not to be compared to it. I, Wisdom [from God], make prudence my dwelling, and I find out knowledge and discretion."

It is not hard for me to believe verse 11. As I mentioned above, the world highly values God's wisdom. They often confuse it with intelligence, but they value it. I have been in the consulting profession for more than twenty-five years, and I have seen firsthand how wisdom is valued. Wisdom helps people break down complex problems and provides a clear path to a solution. Organizations will pay millions of dollars to those who can bring that type of insight. I've witnessed it and been the beneficiary of it many times in my career.

Verse 12 also provides a nice nugget of truth. "I, Wisdom [from God] make prudence my dwelling." One definition of prudence is good or sound management. So, to restate the verse, I, Wisdom (from God), make good management my dwelling. How important is good management to the success of any endeavor? The scripture tells us that wisdom produces prudence or the insight to manage well. We should seek wisdom as diligently as we seek training in the latest management fad. Management training is valuable, and we must seek to learn and grow in our understanding. It is part of developing our skills. But seeking wisdom is even more important because God will show you how to turn the knowledge provided in your training into a good and sound management approach for the situation you are dealing with. The training class provides knowledge of the *what*; wisdom provides the *how*.

There is no shortage of the *what* in the world today because everyone has an opinion. It can be obtained in a class, in white papers, and in searching the web. However, the *how* is what everyone wants to know and highly values. Without the *how* all I have is an idea. It could be a good one, but it must be implemented for it to be impactful. This truth also holds for a vision you may get from God. He may give you a vision that shows you His desire for a situation, but you will need His wisdom to order your steps to realize the vision.

How do we use what we know and the resources at our disposal to deliver a good outcome? People and organizations pay handsomely for the *how*. God's wisdom provides the *how*, and it is God's desire to give it to the righteous. Just as we did with righteousness, let's look at what the benefits of wisdom are according to the scriptures:

- Proverbs 1:7 (AMP): "The reverent *and* worshipful fear of the Lord is the beginning *and* the principal *and* choice part of knowledge [its starting point and its essence]; but fools despise skillful *and* godly Wisdom, instruction, *and* discipline."
- Proverbs 2:4–5 (AMP): "If you seek [Wisdom] as for silver and search for skillful *and* godly Wisdom

as for hidden treasures, Then you will understand the reverent *and* worshipful fear of the Lord and find the knowledge of [our omniscient] God."

- Proverbs 3:13 (AMP): "Happy (blessed, fortunate, enviable) is the man who finds skillful *and* godly Wisdom, and the man who gets understanding [drawing it forth from God's Word and life's experiences]."

- Proverbs 4:5–9 (AMP): "Get skillful and godly Wisdom, get understanding (discernment, comprehension, and interpretation); do not forget and do not turn back from the words of my mouth. Forsake not [Wisdom], and she will keep, defend, and protect you; love her, and she will guard you. The beginning of Wisdom is: get Wisdom (skillful and godly Wisdom)! [For skillful and godly Wisdom is the principal thing.] And with all you have gotten, get understanding (discernment, comprehension, and interpretation). Prize Wisdom highly and exalt her, and she will exalt and promote you; she will bring you to honor when you embrace her. She shall give to your head a wreath of gracefulness; a crown of beauty and glory will she deliver to you."

- Proverbs 11:2 (AMP): "When swelling *and* pride come, then emptiness *and* shame come also, but with the humble (those who are lowly, who have been pruned or chiseled by trial, and renounce self) are skillful *and* godly Wisdom *and* soundness."

- Proverbs 18:4 (AMP): "The words of a [discreet and wise] man's mouth are like deep waters [plenteous and difficult to fathom], and the fountain of skillful *and* godly Wisdom is like a gushing stream [sparkling, fresh, pure, and life-giving]."
- Proverbs 31:26 (AMP): "She opens her mouth in skillful and godly Wisdom, and on her tongue is the law of kindness [giving counsel and instruction]."
- Proverbs 24:3 (AMP): "Through skillful *and* godly Wisdom is a house (a life, a home, a family) built, and by understanding it is established [on a sound and good foundation]."
- Proverbs 24:14 (AMP): "So shall you know skillful *and* godly Wisdom to be thus to your life; if you find it, then shall there be a future *and* a reward, and your hope *and* expectation shall not be cut off."
- Proverbs 3:15–18 (AMP): "Skillful *and* godly Wisdom is more precious than rubies; and nothing you can wish for is to be compared to her. Length of days is in her right hand, and in her left hand are riches and honor. Her ways are highways of pleasantness, and all her paths are peace. She is a tree of life to those who lay hold on her; and happy (blessed, fortunate, to be envied) is everyone who holds her fast."

The Word of God promises that those who walk in skillful and godly wisdom will:

1. Revere and worship the Lord
2. Be happy and blessed
3. Have the ability to understand and discern the challenges around them
4. Be promoted and honored
5. Be humble
6. Speak words that give peace and life
7. Have a stable life, home, and family
8. Be blessed with a long life
9. Be pleasant and peaceful
10. Be fortunate and envied

When you consider these promises and the impact they can have on your life and the lives of those around you, it is not hard to understand why the Word tells us to seek wisdom like rubies, gold, and silver. Wisdom provides us understanding of how to apply our knowledge to solve any personal or professional challenge we are faced with. Wisdom provides the understanding of how to do everything we are tasked with better. We have a promise from the Creator of the universe that He will provide us insight into anything we seek His help on. The Word says we have not because we ask not. It comes back to what I've mentioned many times: what measure will you mete? Will you ask and then believe that God will respond?

That all sounds good, and I hope it is an encouragement to you, but how would you assess your desire for it? If you looked at how much time you spend pursuing gold and silver and how much time you spend seeking God's wisdom, what would that ledger look like? Is there a shifting of time and focus that needs to take place? I am not suggesting you quit your job because you are spending eight to ten hours a day working and not seeking God's wisdom. I am asking, what are you doing with the time you have away from the job? How much of that time is spent reading His Word and seeking His wisdom in prayer?

I continue to work at balancing my time to be more consistent in seeking the things of God in the midst of an often-hectic schedule. His wisdom will show us how to be more efficient and direct our focus so we can spend less time dealing with the challenges of the day. I am setting aside the time, not as a religious activity but because I want to hear from God. I know He speaks, I know He speaks to me, and I need to set aside time to listen. I know I need His guidance and wisdom to successfully deliver on the responsibilities I have. I have seen how valuable and impactful His wisdom is, and I am convinced my success depends on it.

I know that on many occasions, God has provided me with insight and solutions to solve problems that my clients and teams have struggled with. Those solutions have provided great benefits to my clients and provided opportunities for members of my teams to grow in their careers and do work they are passionate about. I have stepped back on many occasions and thought to myself that I am so imperfect, yet God continues to bless me with His wisdom and understanding. How great is His grace.

I can speak from experience that God does reward those who diligently seek Him. I say that not to leave the impression that I spend X hours a day seeking Him. I don't; I am as imperfect as anyone else. However, I continue to work to get better at it, not because I am trying to impress God or anyone else, but because I have experienced God's presence in my life, and I have seen Him work in my life, and I want more of it, and I want to be a blessing to Him. All of that only makes me want to seek Him more, and I must continually work to keep the cares of this world from creeping in and taking away the time I am spending with Him.

James 1:5 (AMP) tells us that if we ask for wisdom, God will provide it: "If any of you is deficient in wisdom, let him ask of the giving God [Who gives] to everyone liberally *and* ungrudgingly, without reproaching *or* faultfinding, and it will be given him."

Spend time seeking God and His wisdom, and He will give it to you. The benefits of that wisdom are extraordinary.

> *He who gains Wisdom loves his own life; he who keeps understanding shall prosper and find good.*
>
> Proverbs 19:8 (AMP)

> *For to the person who pleases Him God gives wisdom and knowledge and joy; but to the sinner He gives the work of gathering and heaping up, that he may give to one who pleases God. This also is vanity and a striving after the wind and a feeding on it.*
>
> Ecclesiastes 2:26 (AMP)

I challenge you to search God's Word and study wisdom. God's wisdom has taken me from where I started to where I am today. I am in no way suggesting that I get it right all the time. I clearly don't, and I never will, but I can get better, and I am working to be better at listening. God's wisdom will cause us to be in positions of greater influence, and as our influence increases, it is even more important for us to seek and walk in His wisdom. From my life experiences, I truly believe the Word when it says that obtaining wisdom is the main thing.

So many times in my life, people have confused wisdom with intelligence. I am not that intelligent, but I desire to bring God's wisdom into everything I do, and when I do, it is impactful. Sometimes it is as clear as the written Word; other times, it is determined in the Spirit. I try to be open to both because I know that my success is based upon God's wisdom. It will determine how effective I am at applying the knowledge I and others have to solve every challenge.

CHAPTER 11

Operating and Leading in Love—the Decision that Releases the Fullness of God's Power and Blessing

I give you a new commandment: that you should love one another. Just as I have loved you, so you too should love one another.

John 13:34 (AMP)

I've saved the most important topic for last. I make this statement not because it is my opinion but because Jesus Himself said so. In Matthew 22:34–40 (AMP), when Jesus was being challenged by religious leaders, He answered their question by telling them what the most important commandment is:

Now when the Pharisees heard that He had silenced (muzzled) the Sadducees, they gathered together. And one of their number, a lawyer, asked Him a question to test Him. Teacher, which kind of commandment is great and important (the principal kind) in the Law? [Some commandments are light—which are heavy?] And He replied to him, You shall love the Lord your God with all your heart and with all your soul and with all your mind (intellect). This is the great (most important, principal) and first commandment. And a second is like it: You shall love your neighbor as [you do] yourself. These two commandments sum up and upon them depend all the Law and the Prophets.

Jesus told them the entire Jewish Law was based on two commandments: (1) love God with all your heart, soul, and mind, and (2) love your neighbor as yourself. In John 13:34–35 (AMP), Jesus plainly tells us how important love is: "I give you a new commandment: that you should love one another. Just as I have loved you, so you too should love one another. By this shall all [men] know that you are My disciples, if you love one another [if you keep on showing love among yourselves]."

All will know that we are Jesus' disciples because we have love for one another. They won't *know* that we are His disciples because we go around saying it every day, or because we go to church three times a week, or because we have a Bible study in our house or wear a cross. If that is our approach, they will just hear the annoying distraction of a noisy gong. They will know because of the love we show them. This goes back to a point made earlier in the book: we witness to people about Jesus by loving them as Jesus loves us, not by preaching to them about Jesus. If you love them long enough, you will get the opportunity to tell them about Jesus because they will notice there is something different about you, and they will know you care for them, so they most likely will ask.

Paul tells us in 1 Corinthians 13:1–3 (AMP) that no matter what we do, if we are not doing it in love, then it is of no value.

If I [can] speak in the tongues of men and [even] of angels, but have not love (that reasoning, intentional, spiritual devotion such as is inspired by God's love for and in us), I am only a noisy gong or a clanging cymbal. And if I have prophetic powers (the gift of interpreting the divine will and purpose), and understand all the secret truths and mysteries and possess all knowledge, and if I have [sufficient] faith so that I can remove mountains, but have not love (God's love in me) I am nothing (a useless nobody). Even if I dole out all that I have [to the poor in providing] food, and if I surrender my body to be burned or in order that I may glory, but have not love (God's love in me), I gain nothing.

Paul is telling us we can do all sorts of good things, but if we are not doing those things motivated by love, it comes to nothing. For example, if I give everything I have to the poor so that people will glorify me, I've done nothing of real value. How can that be? That seems like a pretty harsh statement. To understand it, we need to understand how God defines love.

One of the biggest hurdles to operating in love is our understanding of what love is. Our culture has so distorted what love is that if we don't get the answer from the source of love, God, we have little to no chance of demonstrating and giving true love. The Bible says that God is a Spirit and God is love. God's love is spiritual. It is not of the flesh (body) or the soul.

Through movies, music, and books, our entertainment-based culture has created the idea that love is based on feelings (soul) and physical attraction (body). We are bombarded with movies, music, and books about people falling in and out of love. While many of the stories may be entertaining, rarely do they portray love as God does. But if you don't have a relationship with God, how could you understand the spiritual aspects of love?

As defined by our culture, love is self-centered and often fleeting. A famous line in the climactic scene of a movie that is viewed by many as being the bell weather of romance and love comes to mind. I'm sure many of you are familiar with the famous line from the movie *Jerry Maguire* when Tom Cruise says to Renée Zellweger in the critical scene where he declares his love for her, "You complete me."

So many see that as a poignant and romantic thing to say, and it may be. However, when you step back and examine the statement, you realize how selfish it really is. I need *you* to complete *me*. "I need you to meet a need for me. I'm not looking to meet your need or to make a commitment to you." It comes as no surprise that our culture's view of something is completely from the *me* perspective.

It also comes as no surprise that God's definition of love is exactly the opposite of what is portrayed by popular culture. His definition of love is about giving and not to oneself. "For God so loved the world He gave…" God made a willful decision to put others ahead of Himself no matter the cost. Loving others as God loves us is a tremendous challenge. It means we are to put others ahead of ourselves, which is exactly the opposite of what our culture constantly tells us: "We must take care of number one, and we love someone based on how they make us feel."

God's definition and example of love mean we are to look to meet the needs of others and potentially receive nothing in return. Even more challenging, it means we must love people we don't even like. That is impossible to do if we take the world's view of love and base it on how we feel about someone.

Love, as God defines it, is a *decision,* and like everything else that God has for us, we must do it by faith. Why do I say that? Because your love for others may never be reciprocated. We must realize that and keep loving no matter what. God does. How many people never return God's love? Sadly, more don't than do. Love is the most important thing; love God and love people. The Bible makes it clear that we can't have the impact the Lord desires for us in our calling without operating in love.

A few years ago, I was given a new level of leadership, and as I was preparing to take on the role by spending time in prayer, I asked God what I needed to learn to lead in this new role effectively. He responded with an answer I did not expect and quite frankly surprised me because I knew at the time I was not knowledgeable enough in the area to do what He asked. He challenged me to look at all my decisions through the lens of love. A few weeks after hearing this in my spirit, I found the scripture that confirmed it, almost verbatim.

> *Let everything you do be done in love (true love to God and man as inspired by God's love for us).*
>
> 1 Corinthians 16:14 (AMP)

We can't love with God's love unless we understand God's love for us. Love is not a concept the business world talks about much, and a lot of that has to do with the skewed view the world has about love, being purely physical and emotional. Yet I am convinced that operating in God's love will be the number one thing that distinguishes followers of Christ from others in the world of business. The Bible clearly says that, but it took me longer than I would like to admit before I really got it.

However, it is easy to see the importance of it in the realm of business. It is impossible to act in greed or in our own self-interest if we use God's love as a criterion for our decisions. If we walk in biblical love, we have the well-being of others as our first priority. Diversity and inclusion are big topics of discussion in the world of business today. Yet if we are walking in God's love, it becomes a nonissue.

God values everyone the same. He created each of us to be unique and yet to operate as one body, the body of Christ. If we are following God and walking in His love, how could we not value everyone just as He does? How could we not recognize the value of considering everyone's perspectives and opinions when defining new or enhancing existing products or services?

Valuing someone's opinion does not mean agreeing with it or even using it. But love shows respect to others by listening and taking the time to understand their perspective. That doesn't apply just to those who agree with you or who are non-confrontational. It applies to those who get under your skin, those who question all your decisions, and those who constantly tell you why something isn't going to work. I think you would agree that if love was based on a feeling, you would never love them. You need to make love the number one thing and make a decision to show them love, God's love.

The lack of God's kind of love being displayed has become an epidemic. We see far too many examples of people hating anything and anyone they don't agree with. That is what our political leaders and media pundits teach and promote. It is their industry. We wonder why our government is so divided. Part of it is because many (especially our younger generations) in society today don't know that we can disagree with someone and do it in love. Why? Because so many leaders model a behavior that if we disagree with someone, we must also hate them. That is not what they say with their words, but it is what they demonstrate with their actions. It is evil.

People have not been taught to separate someone's opinion or actions from who the person is. God's love can. After all, He gave the best He had even though we were sinners. Even though He was not happy with our actions, He gave. His model is that He decided to love us even though we didn't love Him. Our world needs to see that kind of love, and the only ones who can consistently show that to them are you and me, those who follow Jesus and are led by the Holy Spirit.

In the world of business, we look at metrics like profit, risk, and revenue. They are all good things and must be considered, but if we don't factor love in as a criterion for making decisions in those areas, we will be making less-than-optimal decisions. A love-focused view will deliver on the two business objectives we've based much of our discussion around.

1. Provide goods and services that will allow a community to flourish
2. Serve employees by providing them with opportunities to express at least a portion of their God-given identity through meaningful, creative work

Both of those goals are focused on a ministry to others, not us. A focus on the common business key performance metrics in the absence of love can lead to greed, to self-promotion, to self-preservation, in other words, behaviors that destroy exactly what one is trying to build and protect. How many times have we seen a company make a decision that polluted the environment and damaged the community just to increase profit? Those decisions were not made in love. They were made with self-preservation in mind. The leaders may have gotten away with it for years, but when their decision was finally brought to light through the damage it caused, they were sued and lost tens and hundreds of millions of dollars. This, in turn, impacted the financial well-being of countless employees and their families, not to mention the environment and community. Those types of decisions are obviously made in the self-interest of the decision-makers and not in love with a view of how it impacts the community and their colleagues.

Furthermore, decisions made completely in the absence of God's love are often fear-based and do not apply the principles we have discussed in this book. It will take strength to make and stand on decisions made in love. You may be viewed as weak because your objective is to love others, not control them. Walking in love does not mean that you are "soft" and unable to make the tough decisions. That is what the world wants others to believe. Many years ago, I heard it said that because basketball star David Robinson was a Christian, he didn't have the "killer instinct" required to win. He was too nice, and the team couldn't win with him as a leader.

They meant he was too weak or soft as a competitor. Well, he went on to win a couple of NBA championships, was a ten-time NBA All-Star, a two-time league MVP, and an NBA Finals MVP. Pretty good for someone who is soft and can't lead. I don't criticize folks who have this viewpoint. If their understanding of love is shaped by our culture, then I'm not sure what other conclusion one could come to. Putting the interest of others ahead of your own and treating competitors with respect is viewed as soft by some because they don't know any better.

God's idea of love is many things, but weakness is not one of them. Do you think Jesus' act of love at the cross was an act of weakness? Hardly! Weakness would have been to call down a legion of angels to remove His burden. He could have done that. It would've been an act of self-preservation, an act of self-promotion. The stakes were high; His life, our future. He endured both a level of physical and spiritual pain that we cannot comprehend.

To make matters worse, He knew how horrible the suffering would be. It wasn't just physical; it was spiritual, as well. He knew He would be going into hell and would be separated from the Father for the first time. Enduring the pain of having all sin placed on Him, He remained focused on His goal of releasing God's love to all who would receive it. It looked to all that He had failed, yet three days later, God exalted Him above all. What a powerful example and lesson of how God's love prevails. Walking in God's love will cost you something:

1. It could cost you short-term advancement or financial benefit
2. It could cost you your reputation with some
3. It could allow some to temporarily take advantage of you
4. It could require you to make difficult decisions you would prefer not to make

As I have contemplated this in thought and prayer over the past few years, it has become very clear to me that it is impossible to consistently achieve the two goals we described for business without focusing on walking in love. Walking in love protects me from slipping into greed or focusing on self-interests. Viewing my role in business as a calling means I want my business or influence to grow so I can bless more people, not just exalt me and my bank account. If I am motivated by love, then I am not making a show of it. I am not exalting myself or boasting of my virtue.

As we have already discussed, the Word tells me that God will exalt me in His timing. If I believe that, then I am not worried about how exposed I might feel by walking in love with those who are not doing the same in return. In 1 Corinthians 13:4–8 (AMP), Paul provides God's definition of love:

> *Love endures long and is patient and kind; love never is envious nor boils over with jealousy, is not boastful or vainglorious, does not display itself haughtily. It is not conceited (arrogant and inflated with pride); it is not rude (unmannerly) and does not act unbecomingly. Love (God's love in us) does not insist on its own rights or its own way, for it is not self-seeking; it is not touchy or fretful or resentful; it takes no account of the evil done to it [it pays no attention to a suffered wrong]. It does not rejoice at injustice and unrighteousness, but rejoices when right and truth prevail. Love bears up under anything and everything that comes, is ever ready to believe the best of every person, its hopes are fadeless under all circumstances, and it endures every-thing [without weakening]. Love never fails [never fades out or becomes obsolete or comes to an end]. As for prophecy (the gift of interpreting the divine will and purpose), it will be fulfilled and pass away; as for tongues, they will be destroyed and cease; as for knowl-edge, it will pass away [it will lose its value and be superseded by truth].*

From the scripture above, we discover the attributes of love. Love:

1. Is patient
2. Is kind
3. Is never envious
4. Never boils over with jealousy
5. Is not boastful or vain
6. Is not conceited
7. Is not rude
8. Does not act unbecomingly
9. Does not insist on its own way
10. Is not touchy
11. Is not fretful
12. Is not resentful
13. Pays no attention to a wrong suffered
14. Does not rejoice in injustice
15. Rejoices when right and truth prevail
16. Holds up under everything
17. Believes the best in all people
18. Never fails.

Do you want to know if you are walking in love? How do you measure against this checklist across your network of relationships? These are the attributes of a believer walking in God's love. As we continue to grow in our relationship with God, these attributes should continue to mature and manifest in all our relationships. Scanning this list, it is easy to see how applying these attributes to our relationships would produce a strong network of colleagues and friends who are committed to us and our success.

What type of followership would you create if you consistently exhibited these attributes in all circumstances, in the face of every challenge? From experience, it produces a network of individuals who constantly rally around you and are willing to go the extra mile to help you succeed. Many times in my career, I have had to ask colleagues to make personal sacrifices to help the team deliver for a client. I am humbled to know that in many cases, they made the sacrifice just because I was the one asking. I believe that was because I have tried to walk in the God kind of love throughout my career, and as a result, they didn't feel as though I was trying to take advantage of them.

After studying this, what God was asking me to do as leader became clearer. When He said, "Make all decisions through the lens of love," He was telling me not to make decisions based on how they benefited me or to right a perceived wrong done to me but based on how they would benefit others. He was telling me not to make decisions that promote me or my success. He wanted me to take my focus off me and let God cover me when I feel exposed by operating in love. He showed me I must focus on the needs of others. He promised He would exalt us in His time. To believe that, we must truly believe that God loves us and that His love toward us is not based on anything we have done. There are no degrees of God's love; He never withholds it. It is always there in full; we must receive it by faith.

God is love, and He so loves us that He gave us His best, His Son, so that He could have a relationship with us. He chose to have a relationship with us, not based on what we could do for Him or how we make Him feel, but so He could bless His children. He demonstrated sacrificial love toward us before we ever made a move in His direction.

After we accepted Jesus as our Savior, He didn't love us more. He is more pleased with us because we now have a relationship with Him. But He does not love us one bit more than He did when we were living in sin apart from Him. God loves those who blaspheme and refuse to accept Jesus as their Lord and Savior just as much as He loves those who have been diligently seeking and serving Him for decades. He loves us, He has given us His best, and He desires to continue to be in relationship with us and bless us so that we can share His love with others. No matter what we've done or what we will do, His love and commitment toward us will never change.

We talked about faith in a previous chapter, and we can put a final point on it here. Ultimately, our thirty-, sixty-, or one-hundred-fold return on our faith is based on our faith in God's love for us. If we think we have to perform for God to love us, then we have a religious view, and we will constantly work to try to earn His love. If we trust in our abilities and not God's love, we will spend precious energy chasing something we already have. We must develop our faith in His decision to love us before we even accept Him and His sacrifice. How wonderful.

Once we truly begin to grasp this truth, it is much easier to believe God's promises are for us, not because we're "good enough" or because we have to do enough to earn them, but because God loves us perfectly, and He perfectly displays the attributes of love toward us that Paul described above. We can trust His love.

As I continued to develop my understanding of how to bring God's love to the workplace, I recognized a few things. I saw that these attributes are actions, behaviors, and conditions of the heart. As I continue to strive to understand how to make all decisions through love, this is a great checklist for me to evaluate the motivation of my actions and decisions. Am I truly looking at how the decisions impact others or just how they impact me? Am I conceited? Am I boastful? Am I touchy? Am I rude? Am I patient? Am I kind? Do I hold a grudge? How do my decisions display these attributes?

How powerful would it be to consistently bring the positive aspects of these attributes to work with us each day as we develop our professional networks? We don't have to worry about getting the credit or the new position. Why? Because God says in His Word that love never fails. When we walk in God's kind of love (sacrificial), He has our backs.

If I walk in love in every situation, the outcome will never be failure. Do we, can I, really believe that? If so, then many of the other attributes listed above become much easier to display. If I'm not afraid of someone having an advantage over me, would I be resentful, fretful, touchy, conceited, boastful, jealous, or envious? Fear drives that bad behavior, not love. First John 4:18 says that perfect love casteth out all fear. An understanding of God's love for us, as well as God's love in us, will cast out all fear. What an amazing statement and one that really requires some meditation. If we believe that God loves us and His promises are for us, then what do we have to fear? If I can make decisions based on love, then I don't need to fear making the decisions nor the consequences of making them.

Want to drive out fear? Walk in love. Have faith in God's love for you. God has guaranteed in His Word that love will never fail. Never. That implies there is an assurance, possibly a protection, when walking in love. Philippians 1:9–11 (AMP) confirms it:

> *And this I pray: that your love may abound yet more*
> *and more and extend to its fullest development in*

knowledge and all keen insight [that your love may display itself in greater depth of acquaintance and more comprehensive discernment], So that you may surely learn to sense what is vital, and approve and prize what is excellent and of real value [recognizing the highest and the best, and distinguishing the moral differences], and that you may be untainted and pure and unerring and blameless [so that with hearts sincere and certain and unsullied, you may approach] the day of Christ [not stumbling nor causing others to stumble]. May you abound in and be filled with the fruits of righteousness (of right standing with God and right doing) which come through Jesus Christ (the Anointed One), to the honor and praise of God [that His glory may be both manifested and recognized].

This scripture confirms that walking in love can protect us from falling and causing others to stumble. "So that you may surely learn to sense what is vital, *and* approve *and* prize what is excellent *and* of real value." How important is that to operating successfully in the business world? How crucial is this to making good decisions in confusing and stressful situations? This scripture tells me if I am walking in love, I can find the right path in very tough situations filled with strife while those around me are fretful and fearful. Furthermore, others value and recognize the confidence and peace that come when walking in God's love. That peace produces results that bless all those involved. People will want to follow you. Consequently, you will find yourself being given positions of more and more influence because of it.

As we have discussed previously, the more influence you get, the more people you can help, but also the more people you can hurt if you misuse the influence given to you. While this is intuitively obvious, we see in the news almost daily how people misuse or violate the influence their position provides them. When you take a hard look as to why, you can trace it in some form to not operating in love and responding to fear. God's love in us and operating through us is our protection. Selfish acts are not motivated by love, greed is not motivated by love, and operating in fear is not motivated by love.

> *Above all things have intense and unfailing love for one another, for love covers a multitude of sins [forgives and disregards the offenses of others].*
>
> 1 Peter 4:8 (AMP)

> *Whoever loves his brother [believer] abides (lives) in the Light, and in It or in him there is no occasion for stumbling or cause for error or sin.*
>
> 1 John 2:10 (AMP)

Love protects us from and covers sin. Jesus' act of love toward us on the cross has covered all our sins forever. But according to these scriptures, our love toward others also has power to cover our sins. None of us are perfect. We make mistakes, we sin, and that sin impacts those around us and our relationships with them. When we confess it, God forgives us. And even though it does not impact our relationship with Him, it can still impact our relationships with those around us. First Peter 4:8 tells us that if we continue to love those around us, love will cover our sins and help restore those relationships our sinful acts may have impacted. Doing the best we can to consistently demonstrate God's love to those around us will keep the relationships from being destroyed even when we mess up. Similarly, our love toward others will cause us to forgive when others sin against us.

It is hard, maybe impossible, to sin against someone if you are walking in love. First John 2:10 confirms that loving our brothers will help prevent us from sinning. This truth is not hard to understand. All sin is based on selfishness (a form of fear); love is not. Love is based on giving to others. When we operate in God's love, we cannot operate in sin. Each thought, each act we take, is either love-based or sin-based (selfish). I don't think there is anything in the middle. What God told me to do with respect to the business decisions I needed to make applies to every area of my life. For me to love others as I love myself, I must put their well-being first. First Corinthians 13:13 (AMP) tells us again that love is the most important thing:

> And so faith, hope, love abide [faith—conviction and belief respecting man's relation to God and divine things; hope—joyful and confident expectation of eternal salvation; love—true affection for God and man, growing out of God's love for and in us], these three; but the greatest of these is love.

If we are going to have a significant impact in the business world, then it is important for us to have faith, but faith without love is powerless; we must operate in love. It is the most important thing and why God led me to view all decisions through love. I am not anywhere close to where I want to be, but I am now aware and have it as a focus. It has caused me to make some decisions I would have preferred not to make, but I know that if I act in love, no matter the circumstances, I will not fail. The results may not always be what I expect in the short term, but I know I will not fail when walking in love. Because of that, I can walk in peace through all the turmoil that comes at me. Colossians 3:14–15 (AMP) tells us:

> *And above all these [put on] love and enfold yourselves*
> *with the bond of perfectness [which binds everything*
> *together completely in ideal harmony]. And let the*
> *peace (soul harmony which comes) from Christ rule*
> *(act as umpire continually) in your hearts [deciding*
> *and settling with finality all questions that arise*
> *in your minds, in that peaceful state] to which as*
> *[members of Christ's] one body you were also called [to*
> *live]. And be thankful (appreciative), [giving praise to*
> *God always].*

Walking in love can provide peace and act as an umpire to settle questions. How important is that in the turmoil and ambiguity that surrounds us daily as we operate in our profession? How many decisions do you make that you've not had to make in the past? What kind of angst (fear) does that cause? Putting on God's love can provide that umpire for you through the Holy Spirit, so you will know which direction to go with respect to the decision at hand. It provides a peace and removes the fear associated with the decision, but it requires a willful act on our part. The scripture says to put on; it does not say wait until it falls on us. It is a willful act on our part. Love is a decision and an action, not a feeling.

Finally, the following scriptures provide the witness God wants us to bring to the world:

"By this shall all [men] know that you are My disciples, if you love one another [if you keep on showing love among yourselves]."

John 13:35 (AMP)

If I [can] speak in the tongues of men and [even] of angels, but have not love (that reasoning, intentional, spiritual devotion such as is inspired by God's love for and in us), I am only a noisy gong or a clanging cymbal.

1 Corinthians 13:1 (AMP)

You want to have a strong witness, so walk in love. Let God love people through you. The scripture tells us if we do that, people will know we represent something different and that we represent God. That it is the key to long-term success in business. As we grow in our understanding of how to walk in love, God can and will release more resources to us to love others with, thereby helping the community to flourish and providing employees with opportunities to express at least a portion of their God-given identity through meaningful, creative work.

I would like to close with a few personal final thoughts for consideration:

1. God is using and will use business to transfer the wealth of the wicked to His people so they can use those resources to demonstrate His love to a hurting world.
2. God is raising up a new generation of business leaders who have this vision and will drive tre-

mendous innovation in the marketplace to bless others.

3. The witness in the marketplace will not be about folks "witnessing" to people in the traditional sense. Rather, it will be about believers walking in the power of God's Holy Spirit, in His wisdom, and full of His love helping society, their employees, and their colleagues to prosper.

Our world is crying out for businesses to provide this type of impact. It is even discussing some of the same concepts in its management training (servant leadership, for example). It is just looking in the wrong places to find answers. We can be the light that brings a "new" understanding to the world. We can operate successfully in the business world by walking in the power of the Holy Spirit, using God's principles of faith, wisdom, and love to bless all those around us. It is radical, and it is a ministry unique to those who are called to the business world. It is my prayer that this book has helped develop that vision in you and strengthened your commitment to spend time seeking God to understand more fully the impact you can make operating in the vocation God has planned for you. I close with 1 Corinthians 16:13–14 (MSG): "Keep your eyes open, hold tight to your convictions, give it all you've got, be resolute, and love without stopping."

FINAL THOUGHTS

It is my prayer that the concepts presented in this book have helped increase your faith and expand your vision of what it means to have a calling of ministry in the world of business. It is not a misuse of spiritual gifts to apply them in the marketplace, so don't let the enemy deceive you. If God called you to your position and has given you a vision, then learning how to walk in all He has provided to achieve success and bless others is something the enemy hates and God desires.

Be bold, not boastful. Learn of and believe God's promises and humbly receive His grace and blessings. The world so needs godly leaders in government and industry to envision and deliver products and services that bless our communities. Be radical in the execution by displaying God's love to all and in all that you do. Most importantly, do not be afraid to bring your whole self—body, soul, and *spirit*—to your profession. When you do, you will be partnering with God to bless your colleagues, clients, customers, and communities as you powerfully perform a ministry that is unique to those called to the business world.

ENDNOTES

1   Keller, Timothy. *Every Good Endeavor: Connecting Your Work to God's Work*. New York: Riverhead Books, 2014.

2   Warren, Rick. *The Purpose Driven Life: What on Earth Am I Here For?* Grand Rapids: Zondervan, 2008.

3   Van Duzer, Jeffrey B. *Why Business Matters To God (And What Still Needs To Be Fixed)*. Downers Grove, Illinois: IVP Academic, 2010.

4   Collins, Jim. "Level 5 Leadership: The Triumph of Humility and Great Resolve," *Harvard Business Review*, v. 79 (February 2001): 66–76, 175.

5   Maxwell, John. *The 21 Irrefutable Laws of Leadership*. Nashville: Thomas Nelson, 2007.

Printed in the USA
CPSIA information can be obtained
at www.ICGtesting.com
JSHW011950080124
54977JS00002B/5